THE NEW MERMAIDS

Sejanus his Fall

THE NEW MERMAIDS

General Editors

PHILIP BROCKBANK
Professor of English, York University

BRIAN MORRIS
Lecturer in English, York University

Sejanus his Fall

BEN JONSON

Edited by W. F. BOLTON

ERNEST BENN LIMITED
LONDON

First published in this form 1966
by Ernest Benn Limited
Bouverie House · Fleet Street · London . EC4
© *Ernest Benn Limited* 1966
Distributed in Canada by
The General Publishing Company Limited · Toronto
Printed in Great Britain

CONTENTS

ACKNOWLEDGEMENTS

AS ALL JONSONIANS must, I have depended heavily on the work of C. H. Herford and Percy Simpson, *Ben Jonson* (volumes II, IV, IX, Oxford, 1925, 1932, 1950) for textual and critical information. I am also indebted to the editions by W. D. Briggs (Boston, 1911) and by B. Nicholson and C. H. Herford (London, 1894, in the original Mermaid Series). The list of Further Reading includes a number of my other sources of information and understanding. My teachers and colleagues, from Professor G. E. Bentley to the General Editors, have contributed much to the insights of this edition, but its oversights are entirely my own.

The edition by J. A. Barish (New Haven and London, 1965, in the Yale Ben Jonson Series) reached me too late to be consulted.

INTRODUCTION

THE AUTHOR

BEN JONSON was born a Londoner in 1572, the posthumous son of an impoverished gentleman. His mother married a bricklayer shortly afterwards, and his circumstances in youth were decidedly straitened. Through the intervention of an outsider, however, he had some education at Westminster School under William Camden, who remained a lifelong friend; but he probably did not finish school and certainly did not go on, as most of his contemporaries there did, to Oxford or Cambridge. Instead he was apprenticed, probably in his stepfather's craft, about 1589, remaining in it long enough only to learn he 'could not endure' it. Before 1597 he had volunteered to serve in Flanders where, during a lull in the fighting, 'in the face of both the camps', he met and killed one of the enemy in single combat and returned from no-man's-land with his victim's weapons. The scene is an emblem for his life: the giant figure, a party to neither faction, warring alone in the classical manner before his awed onlookers.

Sometime in the early 1590s he married. By the time he was twenty-five he was playing the lead in Kyd's *Spanish Tragedy* for the theatrical manager and entrepreneur Philip Henslowe. As a writer he may also have composed additions to Kyd's work; he certainly did so for Nashe's satirical *Isle of Dogs*, and was imprisoned for the 'slandrous matter' in it. But already by 1598 Francis Meres listed him in *Palladis Tamia* amongst 'our best for tragedy' along with Kyd himself and Shakespeare. These tragedies, and indeed all the work of his early twenties, have vanished, but in the surviving records the man bursts upon the theatrical scene with characteristic and transforming energy.

In 1598 as well his first great success in comedy, *Every Man in his Humour*, was produced; in this, as in *Sejanus*, Shakespeare played a leading role. Within the same month Jonson killed an actor in Henslowe's company, Gabriel Spencer, in a duel. He pleaded guilty to a charge of felony and saved himself from the gallows only by claiming 'benefit of clergy', that is, by proving his literacy and hence immunity by reading 'neck-verse'. His goods—such as they may have been—were confiscated and he was branded on the thumb. His career was not yet fully under way: in writing of the incident, Henslowe refers to Jonson as a 'bricklayer'.

Still in the same year *The Case is Altered* was acted, once again with great success, and in 1599 or 1600 came *Every Man out of his Humour*, which—although it too enhanced his growing reputation—included in the targets of its satire the diction of some contemporary playwrights, notably John Marston. Marston may have annoyed his older friend by a bungled attempt to flatter him in *Histriomastix* a few months earlier, but he was in any case ready to take very unfriendly revenge for *Every Man out* when, in late 1600, he caricatured Jonson in *Jack Drum's Entertainment*. Jonson countered with *Cynthia's Revels*, Marston with *What You Will*, Jonson with *Poetaster*, all in 1601. Thomas Dekker, previously Jonson's collaborator on the lost tragedy *Page of Plymouth*, came to Marston's aid with *Satiro-mastix*. But Jonson had gone beyond attacking his attackers: his plays, and particularly *Poetaster*, satirized influential men, and he barely escaped prosecution again. He withdrew, not yet thirty years old, from comedy and the popular stage, into the patronage and protection first of Sir Robert Townshend and later Esmé Stewart, Lord Aubigny, to whom he dedicated the fruit of his retirement, *Sejanus*.

Once again Jonson's talent for trouble caused him difficulty with the authorities (see 'History of the Play' below), this time on the pretext of 'popery and treason'—he had become a Catholic during his imprisonment for killing Spencer—and once again powerful friends intervened to save him. Still again in 1604, when he collaborated with his reconciled friend Marston and with George Chapman on the comedy *Eastward Ho!* he was jailed, now for satirizing the Scots, for James I was king. But once more he was let off, and on the whole the accession of James I was of great benefit to Jonson: for this brilliant and learned court he wrote almost all his many masques, delicate confections of erudition and artistry in which he knew no master.

But it is to *Volpone* (1605), *Epicoene* (1609–10), *The Alchemist* (1610), *Bartholomew Fair* (1614) and *The Devil is an Ass* (1616) that we must turn for the central documents of his comic maturity, interrupted only by the tragic (and unsuccessful) *Catiline* of 1611. Jonson had by 1612 become conscious of the scope of his accomplishment, for in that year he began work on a collective edition which would enshrine in an impressive folio the authoritative text. His close connections with the court, doubtless enhanced when he gave up Catholicism about 1610, and the literary self-awareness begot by his huge reading in the classics, in part recorded in his commonplace book *Timber*, led him, unique amongst the playwrights of his age, to take such pains with his *oeuvre*.

Jonson continued writing his masques and non-dramatic poems, but no stage play appeared after *The Devil is an Ass* until *The Staple of News* in 1625. Jonson's fortune declined in the nine years between. He began them with a walking tour to Scotland in 1618, where Drummond recorded their *Conversations*, and with a visit to Oxford in 1619, where the University made him a Master of Arts. He ended them increasingly destitute of health, money and invention. His rule over the 'tribe' that met at the Mermaid was unweakened, but he depended more and more on pensions from Crown and City, especially when he failed to maintain with the self-indulgent Charles I the favour he had found with the scholarly James I.

There followed *The New Inn* (1629), *The Magnetic Lady* (1632), and *The Tale of a Tub* (1633); the first was a disaster the last two did little to mitigate. Apart from a few verses he wrote nothing thereafter (his *English Grammar*, a draft of which perished in the fire that destroyed his library in 1623, probably goes back to a period as Professor of Rhetoric at Gresham College), although his lifelong habit of reading was not broken. He did not complete work on the second folio which was to include his writings since 1612. No child of his survived him, and it fell to his intellectual disciples, the 'Sons of Ben', to be his literary executors.

He died on 6th August, 1637, at the age of sixty-five, and was buried in Westminster Abbey.

THE PLAY

HISTORY OF THE PLAY

Sejanus was first acted in 1603, according to the title-page of the 1616 folio, 'by the King's Majesty's Servants', that is, the King's Men, Shakespeare's company. A note at the end of the play includes as 'the principal Tragedians' Richard Burbage, leading actor of the company, who probably played the title-role; Shakespeare himself, who may have played Tiberius; and John Heming and Henry Condell, who were responsible for the Shakespeare First Folio in 1623. The production took place in the Globe Theatre, as some commendatory verses to the 1605 quarto make clear, and the play was hissed off the stage. Sometime between 1605 and 1616, by which time Jonson could write that the play 'begot itself . . . the love of good men', *Sejanus* enjoyed a successful revival, and in its restored esteem provided a quarry for poets, from Fletcher and Drayton to Milton, who adopted its language. In 1752 Francis Gentleman published an inferior adaptation of the entire play.

Sejanus was entered on the Stationers' Register by Edward Blount in November 1604—about a year after the first performance—and transferred in August 1605 to Thomas Thorp, who published it the same year in quarto. But as Jonson's 'To the Readers' makes clear, the text is not that of the 1603 performance, 'wherein a second pen

has had good share'; he had, out of respect for his erstwhile collaborator, revised the work and published it as entirely his own. Neither
the name of 'the second pen', nor the lines which before the revision
were his 'share', can be identified on present evidence, but the most
probable dramatist was Chapman. It was he who most nearly shared
with Jonson the poetic and political attitudes that would have been
necessary for collaboration, and it was he who contributed by far
the longest of the eight commendatory poems which accompanied
the quarto edition.

   The reason for replacing the collaborative lines may be found in
Jonson's remark to Drummond (*Conversations*, 13) that he was
'called before the Council for his *Sejanus*', a difficulty that he seems
to have overcome; but when, a year later, *Eastward Ho!* gave similar
offence, Jonson and his collaborators, Chapman and Marston, were
imprisoned, and avoided serious punishment only through the
intervention of powerful friends. So, when in 1605 Jonson came to
publish *Sejanus*, he may have decided to save his old friend and cell-
mate further peril by taking full responsibility for the play. No
doubt the most offensive lines by Jonson too were altered for the
published version, although a few hints of what they may have
been remain in the quarto: 'so soon, all best turns, / With
princes, do convert to injuries', which the folio makes innocuous,
'so soon, all best turns, / With doubtful princes, turn deep injuries /
In estimation, when they greater rise, / Than can be answered'
(III, 302–305). On the other hand, the closing sentence of the Argument, a protestation of the loyal intention of the play, appears in the
quarto but not the folio.

SOURCES

In 'To the Readers' Jonson mentioned the two principal sources
for his historical material, Tacitus' *Annals* and Dio Cassius' *History
of the Romans*, the former written in Latin, the latter in Greek. But
he made use of many other sources, and most of them he noted in
the margins of the 1605 quarto, in this fashion:

SABINUS
   Hail ᵃCaius Silius.
SILIUS   ᵇTitius Sabinus, hail,
where the marginal notes read

ᵃ*De* Caio Silio. *vid.* Tacit. Lips. edit. 4°. *Anna.* lib. I. *pag.* II. *lib.* 2.
pag. 28 & 33.
ᵇ*De* Titio Sabino. *vid.* Tac. *lib.* 4. *pag.* 79,

i.e., 'About Caius Silius, see Tacitus, Lipsius' edition, quarto,
Annals, Book I, page 11, Book II, pages 28 and 33. About Titius

Sabinus, see Tacitus, Book IV, page 79'. Sometimes he gives supplementary information; of 'fifty sestertia' (I, 183) he notes '*Monetæ nostræ* 375. *li. vide* Budæum. *de Asse. lib.* 2. *pag.* 64', 'In our money, £375. See Budé, *On the Coin*, Book II, page 64'. But most of the notes refer to sources alone: they include Juvenal, Seneca, Suetonius, Pliny, Horace, and Plautus, but Tacitus and Dio figure most largely. ('To the Readers' and the marginal notes were alike omitted from the 1616 folio.)

Often Jonson followed his sources so closely that he provided something of a verse translation of them. Such, as he pointed out to Drummond (*Conversations*, 18), is the speech III, 407–460, translated from Tacitus' *Annals*, Book IV, chapters 34–35; so is the speech II, 178–185, translated from Lucan's *Pharsalia*, VIII, 489–495, which also survives in a separate manuscript draft.

Not all of Jonson's sources, however, were classical. As he points out in his marginal note to V, 101, he made use of Renaissance scholarship as well, in this case by the editor of the collected works of Tacitus, the Belgian Justus Lipsius (1547–1606). More often he accepted Lipsius' aid without acknowledgement, reproducing material from the Belgian's own marginalia, or (in the note to I, 571) from Lipsius' study *On the Cross*. Similarly, he mentions 'Rhodig' (Ludovico Ricchieri Rhodiginus, author of *Sixteen Books of Old Readings*, 1516) in the note to IV, 309, but is equally indebted to him for the passage beginning IV, 283. And, fittingly, he draws upon Machiavelli, both *The Prince* and the *Discourses on Livy*, although it is Sejanus and those of his ilk who alone voice and approve of Machiavelli's principles. Jonson made his way to his sources through 150 years of classical scholarship in Europe, never hesitant to benefit by the labours of those who went before him.

But if he was scrupulous in his attention to ancient and contemporary authorities, it was in the interest of something other than mere historical accuracy. On the contrary, he reassembled the facts of history to form his dramatic structure, and elaborated on them to make his poetic fabric. The Senate scene of Act III, for example, compresses the aftermath of Drusus' murder from several years into minutes, bringing together the presentation of Nero and young Drusus, the accusation of Silius, the latter's suicide, and the accusation of Cordus. Jonson adds Afer as the accuser, 'borrowing' him in that role from the trial two years later of Claudia Pulchra. He provides Silius' great speech III, 319–339, unrecorded in history, here elaborated from hints in Seneca, Lucan, and Cicero (not noted in the quarto marginalia). And he introduces the counterpoint of Arruntius' commentary, although Arruntius was historically involved in events after the death of Sejanus.

Thus Jonson's first requirement for tragedy, 'truth of argument', implies not only historicity but verisimilitude, the continuity of the dramatic illusion. It obliges him to avoid 'unplayable' action, like the dismemberment of Sejanus, on the stage, and it obliges him equally to support the action he does present by compositional and inventive art. That Jonson is rather more 'historical' outside of Act III is beside the point. Act III reveals him handling history, not, as Hazlitt said, like an 'ancient mosaic', but as a fully plastic medium to be shaped into a new form.

THE NATURE OF THE PLAY

In the 'Apologetical Dialogue' 'To the Reader' concluding *Poetaster* (1601), Jonson wrote 'I will try / If Tragedy have a more kind aspect';

> I, that spend half my nights, and all my days,
>> Here in a cell, to get a dark, pale face,
> To come forth worth the ivy, or the bays,
>> And in this age can hope no other grace—
> Leave me. There's something come into my thought,
> That must, and shall be sung, high, and aloof,
> Safe from the wolf's black jaw, and the dull ass's hoof.
>> (223–239)

In his picture of himself as a laureate poet Jonson anticipates both the classical subject of *Sejanus* and its elevated theme. It is a learned play, at once a response to the success of Shakespeare's *Julius Cæsar* (1599) and a vindication of English erudition.

Jonson had already tried his hand at tragedy: he had written a lost *Richard Crookback* (1602) and planned *Mortimer* (1597), which was to include a chorus; and he had written the *Page of Plymouth* with Dekker, and provided additions to *The Spanish Tragedy*. *Catiline* was yet to come (1611). His *Observations upon Horace his Art of Poetry*, had they survived the fire in his library, would doubtless have made clear the theory behind this extensive body of tragedy; as it is, the address 'To the Readers' contains a valuable and almost unique expression of Jonson's tragic theory prefaced to an example of its practice (the theories in *Timber* and *Conversations* are not directed to a particular play).

Having suggested that the classical chorus cannot accurately be reproduced in a contemporary play, given the theatre and the audience, he goes on to the criteria he considers still relevant for a tragedy: truth of argument, dignity of persons, gravity and height of elocution, fulness and frequency of sentence. The meaning of the first we have already discussed. 'Dignity of persons' refers to social station, not to social behaviour; the characters must be dignitaries. 'Gravity and height of elocution' refers to the most elevated of the three styles of declamation, suitable for noble subjects and learned audiences. 'Sentence' is the rhetorical *sententia*, the generalized sententious aphorism or gnome about the human life and action. The criteria produce a drama often called 'Senecan'.

Yet all of these criteria could have been met within the limits of the historical situation outlined in Jonson's sources, and with this, we have seen, he was not content. For his age, his higher purpose would have been manifest on the title page: *Sejanus his Fall. A Tragedy*. The subject of tragedy for the Renaissance, as for the Middle Ages (cf. Chaucer's *Monk's Prologue*), was the fall of great men. The enormously popular *Mirror for Magistrates*, itself an outgrowth of Lydgate's *Fall of Princes*, contains in one stanza of Thomas Sackville's 'Induction' (1563) a compact version of the theory:

> Lo here (quoth Sorrow) princes of renown,
> That whilom sat on top of Fortune's wheel
> Now laid full low, like wretches whirlèd down,
> Even with one frown, that stayed but with a smile .... (526–529)

Sackville's vision begins as he observes the end of the year and the end of the day:

> And sorrowing I to see the summer flowers,
> The lively green, the lusty leas forlorn,
> The sturdy trees so shattered with the showers,
> The fields so fade that flourished so before,
> It taught me well all earthly things be born
> To die the death, for naught long time may last.
> The summer's beauty yields to winter's blast.
>
> Then looking upward to the heaven's leams
> With night's stars thick powdered everywhere,
> Which erst so glistened with the golden streams
> That cheerful Phoebus spread down from his sphere,
> Beholding dark oppressing day so near:
> The sudden sight reduced to my mind,
> The sundry changes that in earth we find.
> That musing on this wordly wealth in thought,
> Which comes and goes more faster than we see
> The flickering flame that with fire is wrought,
> My busy mind presented unto me
> Such fall of peers as in this realm had be:
> That oft I wished some would their woes describe.
> To warn the rest whom fortune left alive. (50–70)

In these twenty-five lines are exemplified the basic assumptions of idea and image on which Jonson's play is built: the uncertainty of worldly prosperity, the particular tragedies of illustrious men, the

fickle face of Fortune, the analogies of the vegetable year and the
solar day. (In his commendatory poem, Chapman wrote of 'Most
noble Suffolk, who by nature noble, / And judgement virtuous,
cannot fall by Fortune', and one who 'durst to look / A Fortune in
the face', and William Strachey wrote an entire sonnet to conclude
'If men will shun swollen Fortune's ruinous blasts, / Let them use
temperance. Nothing violent lasts'.)

In his opening speech, Sabinus says he and Silius have no 'shift
of faces' (I, 7), no capacity for duplicity, commonly employed in
Tiberius' court 'to raise / . . . a fortune, by subverting theirs' (I, 17–
18). Schemers seek to set themselves high ('raise') on Fortune's
wheel by lowering others on it ('subverting'). Sejanus even has the
appearance of Sackville's Fortune herself: 'but 'tis his frown / That
is all these, where, on the adverse part, / His smile is more. . .'
(I, 209–211), and he is 'the second face of the whole world' (I, 217).
Thereafter the language of the play returns more and more often to
Fortune, the unstable mistress of worldly wealth, and face, the
deceitful aspect of worldly things[1].

In the scene (II, 53f.) between Eudemus and Livia, his cosmetic
attentions to her face accompany a conversation which ends

EUDEMUS . . . your fortune hath prescribed you better
    Than art could do.
LIVIA   Thanks, good physician,
    I'll use my fortune (you shall see) with reverence. (II, 135-137)

Here action and dialogue complement each other. The trivial action
throws into stark relief the horror of the dialogue:

EUDEMUS
    When will you take some physic, lady?
LIVIA   When
    I shall, Eudemus: but let Drusus' drug
    Be first prepared.   (II, 121-123)

In giving physical reality to the image of the deceptive face, and in
juxtaposing this reality with the topic of Fortune, the scene addresses
the controlling concern of the play. Plainly, one climax in the reitera-
ted discussion of Fortune will take place in the scene which is literally
'devoted' to her, the scene in which Sejanus vainly attempts to
placate his 'one deity' and finds that 'Fortune averts her face!'
(V, 186). Here, the vocabularies of face and Fortune coalesce omi-
nously, and Sejanus' reaction is not so impious as merely uncom-

[1] See Act I, 251, 265, 363, 510 n., 574; II, 95, 135, 137, 141, 153, 261, 487;
III, 46, 88, 291, 320f., 502, 513, 588, 740; IV, 3, 45, 53, 68, 117, 169, 264,
272, 310, 384, 431; V, 23, 43, 81, 171f., 211, 236, 320, 366, 390, 436, 499,
700, 705f, 791, 802, 865, 891f.).

prehending. Duped by Macro, he can say 'Fortune, be mine again; thou hast satisfied / For thy suspected loyalty' (V, 366–367).

The repeated references to 'face' intersect not only with those to Fortune, but, as Christopher Ricks has pointed out, with those to other parts of the body: Silius' corporal images of deceit in the opening lines are only the first, and they become increasingly dense in the dialogue until they enter the action, in the beheading of the statue early in Act V, then in its complete destruction, finally in the dismemberment of Sejanus himself. This pattern of word and deed supports two themes in the play: the general one of fleshliness, and the specific one of the body politic. Sejanus' progress from the 'abusèd body' (I, 214) to the dismembered corpse is a microcosm of the fate of Rome.

The cyclic favours of Fortune were recalled to Sackville's mind by the cycles of the seasons and the hours. On these images too Jonson relied for two recurring figures in his play. The vegetative image, appropriately, begins with seeds (I, 119–121) of virtue in Germanicus, whose family are repeatedly described as his 'shoots' (II, 192, 500; IV, 69; especially V, 242f.), as are the opposing favourites of Sejanus: 'Men grow not in the state, but as they are planted / Warm in his favours' (V, 503–504), who abandon him when his fortune turns: 'how the leaves drop off, this little wind!' (V, 620). In a like way, Sejanus is first opposed to the solar cycle: 'Seest thou this, O sun, / And do we see thee after?' (I, 197–198), but appears to unite victoriously with it: 'most happy, and ere / The sun shall climb the south, most high Sejanus' (V, 335–336; cf. II, 385). But the midnight promise of a triumph at dawn is false. 'Sejanus' fall?' / He, that this morn rose proudly, as the sun? / And, breaking through a mist of clients' breath, / Came on as gazed at, and admired, as he / When superstitious Moors salute his light!' (V, 711–715; cf. V, 724); 'For, whom the morning saw so great, and high, / Thus low, and little, 'fore the even doth lie' (V, 905–906).

If the inevitable cycle of months and hours appropriately recalls the changing favours of Fortune, what is man to do? Jonson gives it to Latiaris to suggest the answer: 'It is a noble constancy you show / ... that not like others, / (The friends of season) you do follow fortune. . .' (IV, 115–117). This constancy is an aspect of the virtue which can defeat Fortune. 'Let Fortune give them nothing; but attend / Upon their virtue' (III, 88–89); 'Men's fortune there [in state] is virtue' III, 740); and, in Silius' speech,

> Silius hath not placed
> His guards within him, against Fortune's spite,
> So weakly, but he can escape your grip
> That are but hands of Fortune: she herself
> When virtue doth oppose, must lose her threats. (III, 321–325)

Fortune is inconstant, and constancy must come from man's self.
It had been a topic for writers from the Romans to Jonson's own age,
when his favourite source Justus Lipsius wrote a treatise *De Con-
stantia*, translated by John Stradling as *Two Books of Constancy* in
1594. 'There be two things that do assault this castle of Constancy
in us, false goods, and false evils: I define them both to be, Such
things as are not in us, but about us: and which properly do not
help nor hurt the inner man, that is, the mind.' The virtue of Constancy, then, which can oppose Fortune, is inward ('guards within
him, against fortune's spite'), an aloofness from the external and
material, the inconstant world over which Fortune has dominion.

Lipsius equates virtue with the mind, and Jonson likewise opposes
wisdom to fortune: 'Fortune, thou hadst no deity, if men / Had
wisdom' (V, 736–737). Against this kind of wisdom Lipsius sets
'Opinion': 'Inconstancy is the companion of Opinion, and . . . the
property of it is to be soon changed, and to wish that undone, which
a little before it caused to be done. But Constancy is a mate always
matched with reason.' Jonson's crowd is controlled by opinion: 'the
rout / (That's still the friend of novelty)' (II, 235–236); 'Alas! / They
follow fortune' (V, 801–802). The patriotism of Sejanus' enemies,
who refuse to rise up against him and Tiberius, therefore, is not
merely servile. It is, instead, an expression of virtuous constancy and
a refusal to be fixed to Fortune's wheel. (Machiavelli, on the other
hand, makes adaptability the sovereign defence against Fortune:
Prince, ch. 25.)

Yet Sejanus falls, proving his enslavement to Fortune, and ful-
filling Jonson's promise of a 'Tragedy . . . high, and aloof'. He falls,
not overcome by the powers of good, but overbalanced by the
powers of evil. In a political 'history' play, such a plot would lack
dramatic conflict or purpose. There is no equilibrium between
forces, and no resolution at the end: Macro will follow Sejanus,
Caligula (a 'good' character!) will follow Tiberius. Only as a tragedy
in the sense outlined by Sackville does Jonson's use of history, and
his recreation of it, have dramatic point. The two separate forces in
the play are not opposites or polarities, but two different views of
man's moral role in his universe. There is no conflict between them
because they do not compete for the same things. Confrontation
leaves them both unchanged.

Such a play, a play of ideas prepared to abandon historicity but
not to present conflict, will lack in some of the qualities we would
call dramatic, even theatrical, and Jonson seems to have expected
that it would when he added the lines at the end of *Poetaster*: 'Where,
if I prove the pleasure but of one, / So he judicious be; he shall
b' alone / A theatre unto me' (226–228). The return of favour which
the play enjoyed after its initial failure shows that it proved the

pleasure of more than one, and if it was not because of the dramatic action, it was probably not either only because of its philosophical perfection or learned forms. The excellence of Jonson's tragedy lies partly in the dramatic embodiment of the ideas it examines, and partly in the poetic voice it gives them.

THE VERSE AND ITS SPEAKING

Jonson's Verse Line is iambic pentameter. It is not the language, or even the rhythm, of everyday speech, and the differences between 'artificial' and 'natural' provide him with interesting opportunities for variation, as in the lines 'If not, go, seek him, to come to us—He / Must be the organ, we must work by now' (III, 648–649), where the second line has verse and speech-rhythms in unison, and the first has them in discord. An extreme example of this discord is 'Warning with beating. And because our laws' (V, 852) which to be 'regular' requires stress on the second syllable of the first gerund, and (normal) stress on the first syllable of the second. This kind of licence is most common in the play, and if it implied that Jonson intended the line to read aloud as a 'regular' iambic pentameter, it would mean that the verse would sound most stilted.

But Jonson was far from intending any such thing. On the stage, the line should be 'Wárning with béating. And becáuse our láws', where the natural stresses provide a powerful rhythm (two dactyls and two iambs), albeit an (irregular) four-foot kind. In effect, the line has two accentual versions, one a potential 'regular' one, the other a 'natural', equally rhythmic one. Such lines are very common in the play, although usually, as here, they come before or after a line of rhythmical 'unison'. (Cf. esp. V, 750–752.)

There are other ways in which Jonson brings together artificial and natural rhythms. Often he marks for elision an unstressed syllable, commonly the -ed (past or past participial) suffix in a word like 'return'd', which—in poetry at least—the early seventeenth century admitted as either two syllables or three. In V, 872, on the other hand, an apparently identical case, he needs 'Deformed' to be trisyllabic, and he marks no elision. The former practice is much more frequent than the latter, and in this edition the reader need only pronounce the -ed suffix as he normally does to realize Jonson's intention; the marks of elision have been dropped, and rare cases like 'Deformed' in V, 872, have been shown with a grave accent. Similarly with internal elision; Jonson wrote 'op'ning' to mark as disyllabic what would, in modern British pronunciation, be unambiguously two syllables in any case (some American readers might pronounce all the written syllables in words like this, and will have to take care with this text, where the modern spelling has been restored).

Sometimes, for 'regular' effect, Jonson will need a special pronunciation which he does not mark: 'O, pop'lar rage!' (V, 779), 'And
knew no masters, but ǎffĕctĭŏns' (I, 61). Readers must watch for
such words. Jonson often varied the normal ten-syllable line by
adding an eleventh, unstressed ('feminine ending'): 'Send him to me,
I'll work him. Royal lady' (II, 24). When sometimes the eleventh
syllable was in the middle of the line, he put an apostrophe (omitted
from this edition) between adjacent vowels in the line to prevent
actors from eliding them to achieve 'regularity': 'You carry things
too—let me borrow' a man' (V, 157). And once, to resolve the con-
flicting demands of artificial and natural rhythms, Jonson divided
a word at line-end (II, 361–362; see note).

The verse of *Sejanus* is blank verse, that is, unrhymed iambic
pentameters, but from time to time rhyme is introduced. There
seems to be no general rule governing its use; not as once was
suggested, merely 'strong feeling' alone. Rhyme is used, as it is in
the drama of Jonson's contemporaries, at the ends of acts, scenes,
and even important speeches within scenes. It is used to mark
sententious or gnomic passages, like I, 433–434. (Here and elsewhere, Jonson also employed 'gnomic pointing', double quotation
marks at the beginning of the relevant lines, more often in the quarto
than in the folio; this edition omits them entirely.) It is common in
soliloquies, but not unusual in dialogues, where characters rhyme
with each other (II, 174–175), or launch into rhyme in mid-speech
(III, 623f.). (Modern readers should be careful not to miss rhymes, like
'dignity: by', II, 240–241, or 'deserts: hearts', II, 272–273, which
no longer sound alike.) And once Tiberius rhymes an English line
with a Greek one (II, 329–330). Perhaps the use of rhyme in the
play can best be thought of as an extension of the use of punctuation—'gnomic pointing', italics, points of exclamation and termina-
tion. It is not part of the poetic form in the way that the five-foot
line is, but it is part of the poet's resources for emphasis and em-
bellishment.

In view of the nature of the play, characterization will be more
fully realized in language than in plot; the action is, we have seen,
motivated by philosophical principles and unlikely to afford opportunity for character 'development'. But the language can and does
act to pick out individual traits, not the least amongst the minor
characters. Arruntius has a rhetorical habit of repeating his key
phrase: 'the men, / The men' (I, 86–87); 'they hunt, they hunt'
(II, 411); 'baits, baits' (II, 414); 'the space, the space' (III, 96). The
exchanges between Opsius and Rufus (IV, 98f.) and Macro and Laco
(V, 136f.) are gems of miniature comic characterization. Indeed, it is
such 'touches'—Sejanus' overbearing 'Sir?' (I, 278), Tiberius' aroused
'H'mh?' (III, 515)—that give the most vivid hints of character.

But if language which characterizes the speaker is a minor aspect of the play's poetry, language which characterizes the subject—that is, description and discussion—is a very major one.

Description may characterize the situation in which the speakers find themselves, as in Sejanus' first interview with Eudemus. Here the conversation moves across the rhythm of the verse line like a series of lightning flashes along a range of mountain peaks:

EUDEMUS
    My lord, I'll promise you a private meeting
    This day, together.
SEJANUS   Canst thou?
EUDEMUS   Yes.
SEJANUS   The place?
EUDEMUS
    My gardens, whither I shall fetch your lordship.   (I, 352–354)

The exchange comprises only three full lines, but it compactly describes in its movement the relationship between the less and less hesitant physician and the eager Sejanus, agitated as he approaches his ends.

Another kind of description rehearses a situation outside the speakers, and so the movement of their dialogue cannot by itself achieve it. This description is more nearly narration, of the kind that the Nuntius (a character in the play not involved in its dramatic action, a neutral reciter) uses in the last Act:

    Part are so stupid, or so flexible,
    As they believe him innocent; all grieve:
    And some, whose hands yet reek with his warm blood,
    And grip the part which they did tear of him,
    Wish him collected, and created new.   (V, 886–890)

The power of this brief speech lies not merely in its choice of words —there are passages where the language is even more vivid—but in its structure:

$$
\left\{
\begin{array}{l}
\text{Part are }
\left\{
\begin{array}{l}
\text{so stupid,}\\
\text{or}\\
\text{so flexible,}
\end{array}
\right.
\text{As they believe him innocent;}\\[2ex]
\text{all} \qquad\qquad\qquad\qquad\quad \text{grieve:}\\[2ex]
\text{And some, whose hands }
\left\{
\begin{array}{l}
\text{yet reek with his warm blood,}\\
\text{And grip the part which they did tear}\\
\quad\text{of him,}
\end{array}
\right.\\[3ex]
\qquad\qquad\text{Wish him }
\left\{
\begin{array}{l}
\text{collected,}\\
\text{and created new.}
\end{array}
\right.
\end{array}
\right.
$$

The structure is initially triplex (Part ... believe; all grieve; some
... wish), with further duplex branching of the syntax (stupid or
... flexible; reek ... and grip; collected, and created). In each of the
first three lines the natural pause is in a different place; the fourth
line has no natural pause, and the fifth mirrors the rhythm of the
first, closing the structure. The interplay of the syntactic and rhythmic forms gives the verse an interest additional to that of its subject.

Discussions in the play take place both in exchanges, like those we
have noted, including the speech of Silius (III, 319f.), and in soliloquies. In his speech beginning Act V, Sejanus 'discusses' with himself his new store of power. After the hyperbole of the first nine
lines, he answers his own rhetoric with a challenge: can satiety be
gratification to the ambitious? In the third section of the unilateral
dialogue, he implies that the conflicts of an age when 'The gods, by
mixing in the cause, would bless / Our fortune with their conquest'
would be more appropriate to his heroic stature than the puny resis-
tance of his own Rome, ironically echoing the complaints of his
victims that they live in a decadent time. This argument—the jubila-
tion, the reflection, the superlative concluding arrogance—requires
heightened language:

> Swell, swell, my joys: and faint not to declare
> Yourselves, as ample, as your causes are.
> I did not live, till now; this my first hour:
> Wherein I see my thoughts reached by my power ....

But the very words convey the limitations of their subject, uplifted
though they and it be. 'Swell, swell' recalls the 'swoll'n fortune' of
I, 574 (and of Strachey's commendatory poem) and prepares the
way for the insane dare of 'bless / Our fortune with their conquest'.
The language, then, takes its force not only from its elevation, but
from its pertinence to the subject of the play and from the ghastly
denouement already hinted at in ' 'tis air I tread: / And, at each step,
I feel my advancèd head / Knock out a star in heav'n!' (cf. V, 821).

The play thus lacks 'purple passages' if even the most important
speeches are taken in isolation from the pattern of which they are
part, and this limitation—if the integration of theme and expression
is a limitation—extends as well to smaller units of verse, the kind of
memorable lines or couplets so often quoted out of context from the
works of Jonson's contemporaries. At the end of Act IV, for example,
Terentius concludes yet another cynical conversation with two trivial
conspirators. Yet the line has power of the breath-stopping kind,
power enough and more to justify its place at the end of the penulti-
mate act. The energy comes from the compression of the statement
itself, and from its coherence in terms of both the figurative context
(generally the language of the solar day, particularly the imme-

diately preceding aphorism 'Who, to be favoured of the rising sun, /
Would not lend little of his waning moon?') and the literal situation
(the fading light of Sejanus' last day alive). In such lines the theme,
imagery and dramatic action achieve their fullest and most forceful
union:

>   The night grows fast upon us. At your service.

NOTE ON THE TEXT

TWO EDITIONS OF *Sejanus*, both excellent texts prepared by Jonson himself, appeared in his lifetime: a quarto (Q) of 1605, and a folio (F) collected *Works* of 1616. Both editions underwent press corrections, chiefly Jonson's, at several stages; the F text was set from a corrected Q (see note on IV, 434–438). I have followed the corrected state of F throughout, retaining its punctuation but modernizing spelling. The line-numbers (save V, 542, to the end) follow those of Herford and Simpson (Oxford 1932, 1950), to enable students to refer to the excellent notes and references in that edition.

With few exceptions, I have noted all my deviations from the corrected text of F. I have not followed Jonson's use of italics—usually to set off foreign words, titles, place-names, and the like—or small capital letters, usually in personal names. I have occasionally modernized his initial capitals after non-final punctuation. I have centred marginal stage-directions. I have been sparing in adding or altering stage-directions, but the lists of characters at the beginning of a scene in F are not strictly entrances; rather they include everyone who will speak in the scene. Such lists almost always begin with the name of the character who has the first speech, and—in F—the name does not introduce the speech itself. I have silently supplied these cues from Q. Speakers' names and other abbreviations are silently expanded, and elisions modernized: e.g., *h'would* becomes *he'd*, *h'is* becomes *he's*. A few other conventions are mentioned in the Introduction. Otherwise editorial interventions are in square brackets or mentioned in the notes.

FURTHER READING

See also the books mentioned in the *Acknowledgements.*

Books about Ben Jonson:

Symonds, J. A. *Ben Jonson*, 1886.
Swinburne, A. C. *A Study of Ben Jonson*, 1889 (like the previous book, an enlightening period piece by a man of letters).
Smith, G. G. *Ben Jonson*, 1919.
Dunn, E. C. *Ben Jonson's Art*, 1925.
Palmer, J. *Ben Jonson*, 1934.
Knights, L. *Drama and Society in the Age of Jonson*, 1937.
Tannenbaum, S. A. *Ben Jonson: A Concise Bibliography*, 1938 (Supplement: 1947).
Barish, J. A. *Ben Jonson: A Collection of Critical Essays*, 1963.
Thayer, C. G. *Ben Jonson: Studies in the Plays*, 1963.

Books and Articles about SEJANUS:

Brandes, G. 'Ben Jonson and his Roman Plays', *William Shakespeare: A Critical Study*, 1898.
Briggs, W. D. 'The Influence of Jonson's Tragedy on the XVIIth Century', *Anglia*, XXXV, 1912.
Briggs, W. D. 'Source-Material for Jonson's Plays', *Modern Language Notes*, XXXI, 1916.
Knights, L. C. 'Tradition and Ben Jonson', *Scrutiny*, IV, 1935.
Enright, D. J. 'Crime and Punishment in Ben Jonson', *Scrutiny*, IX, 1941.
Duffy, E. M. T. 'Jonson's Debt to Renaissance Scholarship in Sejanus and Catiline', *Modern Language Review*, XLII, 1947.
Bryant, J. A., Jr. 'The Nature of the Conflict in Jonson's *Sejanus*', *Vanderbilt Studies in the Humanities*, I, 1951.
Honig, E. 'Sejanus and Coriolanus: A Study in Alienation', *Modern Language Quarterly*, XII, 1951.
Bryant, J. A., Jr. 'The Significance of Ben Jonson's First Requirement for Tragedy: "Truth of Argument" ', *Studies in Philology*, XLIX, 1952.
Burton, K. M. 'The Political Tragedies of Chapman and Ben Jonson', *Essays in Criticism*, II, 1952.
Olive, W. J. '*Sejanus* and *Hamlet*', *A Tribute to George Coffin Taylor*, 1952.
Gilbert, A. 'The Eavesdroppers in Jonson's *Sejanus*', *Modern Language Notes*, LXIX, 1954.

Boughner, D. C. 'Jonson's Use of Lipsius in *Sejanus*', *Modern Language Notes*, LXXIII, 1958.

Boughner, D. C. ' "Rhodig" and "Sejanus" ', *Notes and Queries*, New Series, V, 1958.

Boughner, D. C. 'Juvenal, Horace, and *Sejanus*', *Modern Language Notes*, LXXV, 1960.

Hill, G. 'The World's Proportion: Jonson's Dramatic Poetry in "Sejanus" and "Catiline" ', *Stratford-upon-Avon Studies*, I, 1960.

Ornstein, R. *The Moral Vision of Jacobean Tragedy*, 1960.

Boughner, D. C. 'Sejanus and Machiavelli', *Studies in English Literature*, I, 1961.

Ricks, C. '*Sejanus* and Dismemberment', *Modern Language Notes*, LXXVI, 1961.

S E I A N V S

his

F A L L.

A Tragœdie.

Acted, in the yeere 1 6 0 3.
By the K. MAIESTIES
SERVANTS.

The Author B. I.

M ART.

Non hic Centauros, non Gorgonas, Harpyiafq3
Inuenies: Hominem pagina noftra fapit.

L ONDON,

Printed by WILLIAM STANSBY,

M. DC. XVI.

Motto. Not here will you find centaurs, not gorgons and harpies: my
page tells of man (Martial, X.iv, 9–10).

TO THE NO LESS
NOBLE, BY VIRTUE,
THAN BLOOD:
Esmé
LORD AUBIGNÉ.   5

MY LORD,
If ever any ruin were so great, as to survive; I think this be one
I send you: the *Fall of Sejanus*. It is a poem, that (if I well
remember) in your Lordship's sight, suffered no less violence
from our people here, than the subject of it did from the rage   10
of the people of Rome; but, with a different fate, as (I hope)
merit: for this hath outlived their malice, and begot itself a
greater favour than he lost, the love of good men. Amongst
whom, if I make your Lordship the first it thanks, it is not
without a just confession of the bond your benefits have, and   15
ever shall hold upon me.
> Your Lordship's most faithful honourer,
>> BEN. JONSON.

Esmé Lord ʾAubigné. Esme Stuart, Seigneur d'Aubigné (1574–1624),
friend and benefactor of Jonson, who honoured him in *Epigram* 127.

To the Readers.

The following, and voluntary labours of my friends, pre-
fixed to my book, have relieved me in much, whereat (without them) I should necessarily have touched: now, I will only
use three or four short, and needful notes, and so rest.   5
     First, if it be objected, that what I publish is no true poem;
in the strict laws of time. I confess it: as also in the want of a
proper chorus, whose habit, and moods are such, and so
difficult, as not any, whom I have seen since the ancients, (no
not they who have most presently affected laws) have yet come   10
in the way of. Nor is it needful, or almost possible, in these
our times, and to such auditors, as commonly things are
presented, to observe the old state, and splendour of dramatic
poems, with preservation of any popular delight. But of this
I shall take more seasonable cause to speak; in my *Observations* 15
upon Horace his Art of Poetry, which (with the text translated)
I intend, shortly to publish. In the meantime, if in truth of
argument, dignity of persons, gravity and height of elocution,
fulness and frequency of sentence, I have discharged the
other offices of a tragic writer, let not the absence of these   20
forms be imputed to me, wherein I shall give you occasion
hereafter (and without my boast) to think I could better prescribe, than omit the due use, for want of a convenient knowledge.
     The next is, lest in some nice nostril, the quotations might   25
savour affected, I do let you know, that I abhor nothing more;
and have only done it to show my integrity in the story, and
save myself in those common torturers, that bring all wit
to the rack: whose noses are ever like swine spoiling, and
rooting up the Muses' gardens, and their whole bodies, like   30
moles, as blindly working under earth to cast any, the least,
hills upon virtue.

1f *To the Readers . . . reducit opimum* Q (F *omits*)
 2 *following . . . labours* commendatory poems omitted in F
 8 *habit, and moods* behaviour and manner (cf. I, 34–35)
23 *convenient* available   25 *nice* over fastidious (usual in Jonson)
26 *affected* assumed artificially   28 *in those* amongst those

7 *laws of time*. Unity of time, a rule of classical drama requiring the action
  to represent a passage of time no longer than the play takes to present.
  Even with its changes of historical chronology, *Sejanus* includes events
  which took place over eight years (A.D. 23 – A.D. 31).

Whereas, they are in Latin and the work in English, it was
presupposed, none but the learned would take the pains to confer
them, the authors themselves being all in the learned tongues,   35
save one, with whose English side I have had little to do: to
which it may be required, since I have quoted the page, to
name what edition I followed. Tacitus, *Works*, ed. Justus
Lipsius, in quarto, Antwerp 1600. Dio Cassius, *History of
the Romans*, ed. Henri Estienne, folio, 1592. For the rest, as   40
Suetonius, Seneca, etc. the chapter doth sufficiently direct, or
the edition is not varied.

Lastly I would inform you, that this book, in all numbers,
is not the same with that which was acted on the public stage,
wherein a second pen had good share: in place of which I have   45
rather chosen, to put weaker (and no doubt less pleasing) of
mine own, than to defraud so happy a genius of his right, by
my loathed usurpation.

Fare you well. And if you read farther of me, and like, I shall
not be afraid of it though you praise me out.   50

Neque enim mihi cornea fibra est.

But that I should plant my felicity, in your general saying
good, or *well*, etc. were a weakness which the better sort of you
might worthily contemn, if not absolutely hate me for.

BEN. JONSON. and no such.   55

Quem palma negata macrum, donata reducit opimum.

34 *confer* compare
43 *numbers* verses
50 *praise me out* judge me precisely

36 *save one.* Richard Greenway, whose 1598 translation of Tacitus'
   Annals Jonson called 'ignorantly done' (*Conversations*, 18), but seems
   to have followed at least in IV, 399.
51 *Neque enim . . . fibra est.* My heart is not of horn (Persius, *Sat.* I, 47).
56 *Quem palma . . . reducit opimum.* Whom the palm denied sends home
   lean; the palm bestowed, plump (adapted from Horace, *Ep.* II.i, 180–
   181).

The Argument.

Ælius Sejanus, son to Sejus Strabo, a gentleman of Rome, and
born at Vulsinium, after his long service in court; first, under
Augustus, afterward, Tiberius: grew into that favour with the
latter, and won him by those arts, as there wanted nothing, 5
but the name, to make him a copartner of the Empire. Which
greatness of his, Drusus, the Emperor's son not brooking,
after many smothered dislikes (it one day breaking out) the
Prince struck him publicly on the face. To revenge which disgrace, Livia, the wife of Drusus (being before corrupted by him 10
to her dishonour, and the discovery of her husband's counsels)
Sejanus practiseth with, together with her physician, called
Eudemus, and one Lygdus, an eunuch, to poison Drusus.
This their inhumane act having successful, and unsuspected
passage, it emboldeneth Sejanus to farther, and more insolent 15
projects, even the ambition of the Empire: where finding the
lets, he must encounter, to be many, and hard, in respect of
the issue of Germanicus (who were next in hope for the
succession) he deviseth to make Tiberius' self, his means:
and instills into his ears many doubts, and suspicions, both 20
against the Princes, and their mother Agrippina: which Cæsar
jealously hearkening to, as covetously consenteth to their
ruin, and their friends'. In this time, the better to mature and
strengthen his design, Sejanus labours to marry Livia, and
worketh (with all his engine) to remove Tiberius from the 25
knowledge of public business, with allurements of a quiet
and retired life: the latter of which, Tiberius (out of a prone-
ness to lust, and a desire to hide those unnatural pleasures,
which he could not so publicly practise) embraceth: the former
enkindleth his fears, and there, gives him first cause of doubt, 30
or suspect toward Sejanus. Against whom, he raiseth (in
private) a new instrument, one Sertorius Macro, and by
him underworketh, discovers the other's counsels, his means,
his ends, sounds the affections of the Senators, divides,

12 *practiseth* plots (usual in Jonson)   17 *lets* hindrances
25 *engine* ingenuity, trickery (frequent)
33 *underworketh* works secretly

10f.(*being before . . . husband's counsels*). This feature of the historical
   narrative Jonson changed to put the blow before the seduction, but
   overlooked the change when he translated this sentence without altera-
   tion from Lipsius' commentary on Tacitus.

distracts them: at last, when Sejanus least looketh, and is most   35
secure (with pretext of doing him an unwonted honour in
the Senate) he trains him from his guards, and with a long
doubtful letter, in one day, hath him suspected, accused,
condemned, and torn in pieces, by the rage of the people.

This do we advance as a mark of terror to all traitors, and   40
treasons; to show how just the heavens are in pouring and
thundering down a weighty vengeance on their unnatural intents, even to the worst princes: much more to those, for
guard of whose piety and virtue, the angels are in continual
watch, and God himself miraculously working.   45

37 *trains* entices
38 *doubtful* ambiguous
40f. *This do ... miraculously working* Q (F *omits*)

The Persons of the Play.

Tiberius.

Drusus senior.	Sejanus.
Nero.	Latiaris.
Drusus junior.	Varro.
Caligula.	Macro.
Arruntius.	Cotta.
Silius.	Afer.
Sabinus.	Haterius.
Lepidus.	Sanquinius.
Cordus.	Pomponius.
Gallus.	Posthumus.
Regulus.	Trio.
Terentius.	Minutius.
Laco.	Satrius.
Eudemus.	Natta.
Rufus.	Opsius.

Tribuni.

Agrippina. }Livia.
          }Sosia.

Præcones.	Lictores.
Flamen.	Ministri.
Tubicines.	Tibicines.
Nuntius.	Servus.

The Scene.
ROME.

SEJANUS HIS FALL

Act I, [Scene i]

[*The Palace. Enter*] SABINUS, SILIUS

SABINUS
  Hail, Caius Silius.
SILIUS   Titius Sabinus, hail.
  You're rarely met in court!
SABINUS   Therefore, well met.
SILIUS
  'Tis true: indeed, this place is not our sphere.
SABINUS
  No, Silius, we are no good enginers;
  We want the fine arts, and their thriving use,   5
  Should make us graced, or favoured of the times:
  We have no shift of faces, no cleft tongues,
  No soft, and glutinous bodies, that can stick,
  Like snails, on painted walls; or, on our breasts,
  Creep up, to fall, from that proud height, to which   10
  We did by slavery, not by service, climb.
  We are no guilty men, and then no great;
  We have nor place in court, office in state,
  That we can say, we owe unto our crimes:
  We burn with no black secrets, which can make   15
  Us dear to the pale authors; or live feared
  Of their still waking jealousies, to raise
  Ourselves a fortune, by subverting theirs.
  We stand not in the lines, that do advance
  To that so courted point.

[*Enter* SATRIUS, NATTA]

SILIUS   But yonder lean   20
  A pair that do.

[*Enter* LATIARIS]

4 *enginers* schemers
5 *want* lack
6 *Should make* that should make (zero relative, frequent)
7 *shift of faces* duplicity
  cleft tongues for flattery
12 *then* therefore
15f. *which . . . authors* which will force wrongdoers to favour us, who
  know their secrets
17 *jealousies* suspicions (frequent)

11

(SABINUS   Good cousin Latiaris.)
SILIUS
    Satrius Secundus, and Pinnarius Natta,
    The great Sejanus' clients: there be two,
    Know more, than honest counsels: whose close breasts
    Were they ripped up to light, it would be found   25
    A poor, and idle sin, to which their trunks
    Had not been made fit organs. These can lie,
    Flatter, and swear, forswear, deprave, inform,
    Smile, and betray; make guilty men; then beg
    The forfeit lives, to get the livings; cut   30
    Men's throats with whisperings; sell to gaping suitors
    The empty smoke, that flies about the palace;
    Laugh, when their patron laughs; sweat, when he sweats;
    Be hot, and cold with him; change every mood,
    Habit, and garb, as often as he varies;   35
    Observe him, as his watch observes his clock;
    And true, as turquoise in the dear lord's ring,
    Look well, or ill with him: ready to praise
    His lordship, if he spit, or but piss fair,
    Have an indifferent stool, or break wind well,   40
    Nothing can 'scape their catch.
SABINUS   Alas! these things
    Deserve no note, conferred with other vile,
    And filthier flatteries, that corrupt the times:
    When, not alone our gentry's chief are fain
    To make their safety from such sordid acts,   45
    But all our Consuls, and no little part
    Of such as have been Prætors, yea, the most
    Of Senators (that else not use their voices)
    Start up in public Senate, and there strive
    Who shall propound most abject things, and base,   50
    So much, as oft Tiberius hath been heard,

23 *clients* men under another's patronage
29f. *beg . . . livings* plead for condemned men, **to gain** control of them
31 *suitors* suppliants for favours

---

36 Probably one of the rare anachronisms of the play, with reference to
   correcting an inaccurate pocket watch by the more reliable public
   clocks; but possibly 'as his guards observe the sundial or waterclock',
   i.e., closely and often.
37 Turquoise is a stone of changeable colour.
44 Punctuation, and therefore syntax, unclear in Q and F, but explained
   by the Latin source (*primores civitatis*) as 'the leaders of the State'.
48 F has the marginal note *Pedarii*, the Senators who had low office and
   consequently only a silent vote.

Leaving the court, to cry 'O race of men,
Prepared for servitude!' Which showed, that, he
Who least the public liberty could like,
As loathly brooked their flat servility.   55
SILIUS
Well, all is worthy of us, were it more,
Who with our riots, pride, and civil hate,
Have so provoked the justice of the gods.
We, that (within these fourscore years) were born
Free, equal lords of the triumphèd world,   60
And knew no masters, but affections,
To which betraying first our liberties,
We since became the slaves to one man's lusts;
And now to many: every ministering spy
That will accuse, and swear, is lord of you,   65
Of me, of all, our fortunes, and our lives.
Our looks are called to question and our words,
How innocent soever, are made crimes;
We shall not shortly dare to tell our dreams,
Or think, but 'twill be treason.
SABINUS   Tyrants' arts   70
Are to give flatterers, grace; accusers, power;
That those may seem to kill whom they devour.

[*Enter* CORDUS, ARRUNTIUS]

Now good Cremutius Cordus.
CORDUS   Hail, to your lordship.

They whisper

NATTA
Who's that salutes your cousin?
LATIARIS   'Tis one Cordus,
A gentleman of Rome: one, that has writ   75
Annals of late, they say, and very well.
NATTA
Annals? of what times?
LATIARIS   I think of Pompey's,
And Caius Cæsar's; and so down to these.
NATTA
How stands h'affected to the present state?
Is he or Drusian? or Germanican?   80
Or ours? or neutral?
LATIARIS   I know him not so far.

61 *affections* passions (as opposed to reason)
79 *affected* inclined

NATTA
  Those times are somewhat queasy to be touched.
  Have you or seen, or heard part of his work?
LATIARIS
  Not I, he means they shall be public shortly.
NATTA
  O. Cordus do you call him?
LATIARIS   Ay.
                              [*Exeunt* NATTA, SATRIUS]
SABINUS   But these our times   85
  Are not the same, Arruntius.
ARRUNTIUS   Times? the men,
  The men are not the same: 'tis we are base,
  Poor, and degenerate from th'exalted strain
  Of our great fathers. Where is now the soul
  Of god-like Cato? he, that durst be good,   90
  When Cæsar durst be evil; and had power,
  As not to live his slave, to die his master.
  Or where the constant Brutus, that (being proof
  Against all charm of benefits) did strike
  So brave a blow into the monster's heart   95
  That sought unkindly to captive his country?
  O, they are fled the light. Those mighty spirits
  Lie raked up, with their ashes in their urns,
  And not a spark of their eternal fire
  Glows in a present bosom. All's but blaze,   100
  Flashes, and smoke, wherewith we labour so,
  There's nothing Roman in us; nothing good,
  Gallant, or great: 'tis true, that Cordus says,
  'Brave Cassius was the last of all that race'.

          DRUSUS *passeth by* [*with* HATERIUS *and a retinue*]

SABINUS
  Stand by, lord Drusus.
HATERIUS   Th'Emperor's son, give place.   105
SILIUS
  I like the Prince well.
ARRUNTIUS   A riotous youth,
  There's little hope of him.
SABINUS   That fault his age
  Will, as it grows, correct. Me thinks, he bears
  Himself, each day, more nobly than other:
  And wins no less on men's affections,   110

  96 *unkindly* unnaturally (*kind* nature)
      captive enslave

Than doth his father lose. Believe me, I love him;
  And chiefly for opposing to Sejanus.
SILIUS
  And I, for gracing his young kinsmen so,
  The sons of Prince Germanicus: it shows
  A gallant clearness in him, a straight mind,   115
  That envies not, in them, their father's name.
ARRUNTIUS
  His name was, while he lived, above all envy;
  And being dead, without it. O, that man!
  If there were seeds of the old virtue left,
  They lived in him.
SILIUS   He had the fruits, Arruntius,   120
  More than the seeds: Sabinus, and myself
  Had means to know him, within; and can report him.
  We were his followers, (he would call us friends.)
  He was a man most like to virtue; in all,
  And every action, nearer to the gods,   125
  Than men, in nature; of a body as fair
  As was his mind; and no less reverend
  In face, than fame: he could so use his state,
  Tempering his greatness, with his gravity,
  As it avoided all self-love in him,   130
  And spite in others. What his funerals lacked
  In images, and pomp, they had supplied
  With honourable sorrow, soldiers' sadness,
  A kind of silent mourning, such, as men
  (Who know no tears, but from their captives) use   135
  To show in so great losses.
CORDUS   I thought once,
  Considering their forms, age, manner of deaths,
  The nearness of the places, where they fell,
  T'have paralleled him with great Alexander:
  For both were of best feature, of high race,   140
  Yeared but to thirty, and, in foreign lands,
  By their own people, alike made away.
SABINUS
  I know not, for his death, how you might wrest it:
  But, for his life, it did as much disdain
  Comparison, with that voluptuous, rash,   145
  Giddy, and drunken Macedon's, as mine
  Doth with my bond-man's. All the good, in him,
  (His valour, and his fortune) he made his;

143 *wrest* twist, interpret artificially

But he had other touches of late Romans,
That more did speak him: Pompey's dignity,   150
The innocence of Cato, Cæsar's spirit,
Wise Brutus' temperance, and every virtue,
Which, parted unto others, gave them name,
Flowed mixed in him. He was the soul of goodness:
And all our praises of him are like streams   155
Drawn from a spring, that still rise full, and leave
The part remaining greatest.
ARRUNTIUS   I am sure
He was too great for us, and that they knew
Who did remove him hence.
SABINUS   When men grow fast
Honoured, and loved, there is a trick in state   160
(Which jealous princes never fail to use)
How to decline that growth, with fair pretext,
And honourable colours of employment,
Either by embassy, the war, or such,
To shift them forth into another air,   165
Where they may purge, and lessen; so was he:
And had his seconds there, sent by Tiberius,
And his more subtle dame, to discontent him;
To breed, and cherish mutinies; detract
His greatest actions; give audacious check   170
To his commands; and work to put him out
In open act of treason. All which snares
When his wise cares prevented, a fine poison
Was thought on, to mature their practices.
CORDUS
Here comes Sejanus.
SILIUS   Now observe the stoops,   175
The bendings, and the falls.
ARRUNTIUS   Most creeping base!

   [*Enter*] SEJANUS, SATRIUS, TERENTIUS, *etc.*

        They pass over the stage

SEJANUS
I note 'em well: no more. Say you.
SATRIUS   My lord,
There is a gentleman of Rome would buy—
SEJANUS
How call you him you talked with?
SATRIUS   Please your lordship,

150 *speak* describe
167 *seconds* seconders, who support another's plans

It is Eudemus, the physician   180
To Livia, Drusus' wife.
SEJANUS   On with your suit.
Would buy, you said—
SATRIUS   A Tribune's place, my lord.
SEJANUS
What will he give?
SATRIUS   Fifty sestertia.
SEJANUS
Livia's physician, say you, is that fellow?
SATRIUS
It is, my lord; your lordship's answer?
SEJANUS   To what?   185
SATRIUS
The place, my lord. 'Tis for a gentleman,
Your lordship will well like of, when you see him;
And one, you may make yours, by the grant.
SEJANUS
Well, let him bring his money, and his name.
SATRIUS
Thank your lordship. He shall, my lord.
SEJANUS   Come hither.   190
Know you this same Eudemus? Is he learned?
SATRIUS
Reputed so, my lord: and of deep practice.
SEJANUS
Bring him in, to me, in the gallery;
And take you cause, to leave us there, together:
I would confer with him, about a grief.—On.   195
              [*Exeunt* SEJANUS, SATRIUS, TERENTIUS, *etc.*]
ARRUNTIUS
So, yet! another? Yet? O desperate state
Of grovelling honour! Seest thou this, O sun,
And do we see thee after? Me thinks, day
Should lose his light, when men do lose their shames,
And, for the empty circumstance of life,   200
Betray their cause of living.
SILIUS   Nothing so.
Sejanus can repair, if Jove should ruin.
He is the now court-god; and well applied
With sacrifice of knees, of crooks, and cringe,
He will do more than all the house of heav'n   205
Can, for a thousand hecatombs. 'Tis he

195 *grief* ailment
204 *knees . . . cringe* kneeling, bending, bowing

Makes us our day, or night; Hell, and Elysium
Are in his look: we talk of Rhadamanth,
Furies, and fire-brands; but 'tis his frown
That is all these, where, on the adverse part,   210
His smile is more, than e're (yet) poets fained
Of bliss, and shades, nectar—

ARRUNTIUS   A serving boy?
I knew him, at Caius' trencher, when for hire,
He prostituted his abusèd body
To that great gourmand, fat Apicius;   215
And was the noted pathic of the time.

SABINUS
And, now, the second face of the whole world.
The partner of the Empire, hath his image
Reared equal with Tiberius', born in ensigns,
Commands, disposes every dignity,   220
Centurions, Tribunes, heads of provinces,
Prætors, and Consuls, all that heretofore
Rome's general suffrage gave, is now his sale.
The gain, or rather spoil, of all the earth,
One, and his house, receives.

SILIUS   He hath of late   225
Made him a strength too, strangely, by reducing
All the Prætorian bands into one camp,
Which he commands: pretending, that the soldier
By living loose, and scattered, fell to riot;
And that if any sudden enterprise   230
Should be attempted, their united strength
Would be far more, than severed; and their life
More strict, if from the city more removed.

SABINUS
Where, now, he builds, what kind of forts he please,
Is hard to court the soldier, by his name,   235
Woos, feasts the chiefest men of action,
Whose wants, not loves, compel them to be his.
And, though he ne're were liberal by kind,
Yet, to his own dark ends, he's most profuse,
Lavish, and letting fly, he cares not what   240
To his ambition.

ARRUNTIUS   Yet, hath he ambition?
Is there that step in state can make him higher?
Or more? or anything he is, but less?

SILIUS
Nothing, but Emperor.

216 *pathic* sodomite   235 *hard* persistent (or *heard*?)

ARRUNTIUS   The name Tiberius
I hope, will keep; how e'er he hath foregone   245
The dignity, and power.
SILIUS   Sure, while he lives.
ARRUNTIUS
And dead, it comes to Drusus. Should he fail,
To the brave issue of Germanicus;
And they are three: too many (ha?) for him
To have a plot upon?
SABINUS   I do not know   250
The heart of his designs; but, sure, their face
Looks farther than the present.
ARRUNTIUS   By the gods,
If I could guess he had but such a thought,
My sword should cleave him down from head to heart,
But I would find it out: and with my hand   255
I'd hurl his panting brain about the air,
In mites, as small as atomi, to undo
The knotted bed—
SABINUS   You are observed, Arruntius.
ARRUNTIUS
Death! I dare tell him so; and all his spies:
You, sir, I would, do you look? and you.
                    He turns to Sejanus' clients
SABINUS   Forbear.   260

                    [*Enter*] SATRIUS, EUDEMUS

SATRIUS
Here, he will instant be; let's walk a turn.
You're in a muse, Eudemus?
EUDEMUS   Not I, sir.
I wonder he should mark me out so! well,
Jove, and Apollo form it for the best.
SATRIUS
Your fortune's made unto you now, Eudemus,   265
If you can but lay hold upon the means;
Do but observe his humour, and—believe it—
He's the noblest Roman, where he takes—
Here comes his lordship.

                    [*Enter* SEJANUS]

257 *atomi* atoms

---

258 Arruntius likens Sejanus' brain to a tangled cluster of serpents; cf.
Pericles IV.ii, 155, 'beds of eels', and *Othello* IV.ii, 64, 'for foul toads to
knot . . . in'.

SEJANUS   Now, good Satrius.
SATRIUS
    This is the gentleman, my lord.
SEJANUS   Is this?   270
    Give me your hand, we must be more acquainted.
    Report, sir, hath spoke out your art, and learning:
    And I am glad I have so needful cause,
    (How ever in itself painful, and hard)
    To make me known to so great virtue. Look,   275
    Who's that? Satrius— [Exit SATRIUS] I have a grief, sir,
    That will desire your help. Your name's Eudemus?
EUDEMUS
    Yes.
SEJANUS   Sir?
EUDEMUS   It is, my lord.
SEJANUS   I hear, you are
    Physician to Livia, the Princess?
EUDEMUS
    I minister unto her, my good lord.   280
SEJANUS
    You minister to a royal lady, then.
EUDEMUS
    She is, my lord, and fair.
SEJANUS   That's understood
    Of all their sex, who are, or would be so;
    And those, that would be, physic soon can make 'em:
    For those that are, their beauties fear no colours.   285
EUDEMUS
    Your lordship is conceited.
SEJANUS   Sir, you know it.
    And can (if need be) read a learnèd lecture,
    On this, and other secrets. Pray you tell me,
    What more of ladies, besides Livia,
    Have you your patients?   Many, my good lord.   290
EUDEMUS
    The great Augusta, Urgulania,
    Mutilia Prisca, and Plancina, divers—
SEJANUS
    And, all these tell you the particulars
    Of every several grief? how first it grew,

272 *art* medical skill   275 *virtue* ability, power
284 *physic* (medical) treatment, especially cathartic
286 *conceited* witty

285 *colours* are cosmetics, with a pun on military colours.

And then increased, what action causèd that;   295
What passion that: and answer to each point
That you will put 'em.
EUDEMUS   Else, my lord, we know not
How to prescribe the remedies.
SEJANUS   Go to,
You're a subtle nation, you physicians!
And grown the only cabinets, in court,   300
To ladies' privacies. Faith which of these
Is the most pleasant lady, in her physic?
Come, you are modest now.
EUDEMUS   'Tis fit, my lord.
SEJANUS
Why, sir, I do not ask you of their urines,
Whose smells most violet? or whose siege is best?   305
Or who makes hardest faces on her stool?
Which lady sleeps with her own face, a' nights?
Which puts her teeth off, with her clothes, in court?
Or, which her hair? which her complexion?
And, in which box she puts it? These were questions   310
That might, perhaps, have put your gravity
To some defence of blush. But, I enquired,
Which was the wittiest? merriest? wantonest?
Harmless intergatories, but conceits.
Me thinks, Augusta should be most perverse,   315
And froward in her fit?
EUDEMUS   She's so, my lord.
SEJANUS
I knew it. And Mutilia the most jocund?
EUDEMUS
Tis very true, my lord.
SEJANUS   And why would you
Conceal this from me, now? Come, what's Livia?
I know, she's quick, and quaintly spirited,   320
And will have strange thoughts, when she's at leisure;
She tells 'em all to you?
EUDEMUS   My noblest lord,
He breathes not in the Empire, or on earth,
Whom I would be ambitious to serve
(In any act, that may preserve mine honour)   325
Before your lordship.

300 *cabinets* secret receptacles   305 *siege* stool
314 *intergatories* questions   *but* mere
316 *froward in her fit* difficult in temperament
320 *quaintly spirited* having unusual ideas

SEJANUS   Sir, you can lose no honour,
   By trusting ought to me. The coarsest act
   Done to my service, I can so requite,
   As all the world shall style it honourable:
   Your idle, virtuous definitions   330
   Keep honour poor, and are as scorned, as vain:
   Those deeds breathe honour, that do suck in gain.
EUDEMUS
   But, good my lord, if I should thus betray
   The counsels of my patient, and a lady's
   Of her high place, and worth; what might your lordship,   335
   (Who presently are to trust me with your own)
   Judge of my faith?
SEJANUS   Only the best, I swear.
   Say now, that I should utter you my grief;
   And with it, the true cause; that it were love;
   And love to Livia: you should tell her this?   340
   Should she suspect your faith? I would you could
   Tell me as much, from her; see, if my brain
   Could be turned jealous.
EUDEMUS   Happily, my lord,
   I could, in time, tell you as much, and more;
   So I might safely promise but the first,   345
   To her, from you.
SEJANUS   As safely, my Eudemus,
   (I now dare call thee so) as I have put
   The secret into thee.
EUDEMUS   My lord—
SEJANUS   Protest not.
   Thy looks are vows to me, use only speed,
   And but affect her with Sejanus' love,   350
   Thou art a man, made, to make Consuls. Go.
EUDEMUS
   My lord, I'll promise you a private meeting
   This day, together.
SEJANUS   Canst thou?
EUDEMUS   Yes.
SEJANUS   The place?
EUDEMUS
   My gardens, whither I shall fetch your lordship.
SEJANUS
   Let me adore my Æsculapius.   355
   Why, this indeed is physic! and outspeaks

343 *Happily* perhaps

The knowledge of cheap drugs, or any use
Can be made out of it! more comforting
Than all your opiates, juleps, apozemes,
Magistral syrups, or—Begone, my friend,   360
Not barely styled, but created so;
Expect things, greater than thy largest hopes,
To overtake thee: Fortune, shall be taught
To know how ill she hath deserved thus long,
To come behind thy wishes. Go, and speed.   365

                              [*Exit* EUDEMUS]

Ambition makes more trusty slaves, than need,
These fellows, by the favour of their art,
Have, still, the means to tempt, oft-times, the power.
If Livia will be now corrupted, then
Thou hast the way, Sejanus, to work out   370
His secrets, who (thou knowest) endures thee not,
Her husband Drusus: and to work against them.
Prosper it, Pallas, thou, that betterest wit;
For Venus hath the smallest share in it.

          [*Enter*] TIBERIUS, DRUSUS, [*attended*]
                   One kneels to him

TIBERIUS
We not endure these flatteries, let him stand;   375
Our Empire, ensigns, axes, rods, and state
Take not away our human nature from us:
Look up, on us, and fall before the gods.
SEJANUS
How like a god, speaks Cæsar!
ARRUNTIUS   There, observe!
He can endure that second, that's no flattery.   380
O, what is it, proud slime will not believe
Of his own worth, to hear it equal praised
Thus with the gods?
CORDUS   He did not hear it, sir.
ARRUNTIUS
He did not? Tut, he must not, we think meanly.
'Tis your most courtly, known confederacy,   385
To have your private parasite redeem

---

359 *opiates ... apozemes.* Sweet medicine, infusions, concentrated potions.
376 *axes, rods.* The *fasces*, axes with rods tied about them, carried before the
    chief magistrates.
385f. *most courtly ... a name.* It is a most court-like, recognized arrange-
    ment, that a flatterer should restore the name that a prince declines.

What he, in public subtlety, will lose
To making him a name.

HATERIUS   Right mighty lord—

TIBERIUS
We must make up our ears, 'gainst these assaults
Of charming tongues; we pray you use, no more   390
These contumelies to us: style not us
Or lord, or mighty, who profess ourself
The servant of the Senate, and are proud
T'enjoy them our good, just, and favouring lords.

CORDUS
Rarely dissembled.

ARRUNTIUS   Prince-like, to the life.   395

SABINUS
When power, that may command, so much descends,
Their bondage, whom it stoops to, it intends.

TIBERIUS
Whence are these letters?

HATERIUS   From the Senate.

TIBERIUS   So.
Whence these?

LATIARIS   From thence too.

TIBERIUS   Are they sitting, now?

LATIARIS
They stay thy answer, Cæsar.

SILIUS   If this man   400
Had but a mind allied unto his words,
How blest a fate were it to us, and Rome?
We could not think that state, for which to change,
Although the aim were our old liberty:
The ghosts of those that fell for that, would grieve   405
Their bodies lived not, now, again to serve.
Men are deceived, who think there can be thrall
Beneath a virtuous prince. Wished liberty
Ne're lovelier looks, than under such a crown.
But, when his grace is merely but lip-good,   410
And, that no longer, than he airs himself
Abroad in public, there, to seem to shun
The strokes, and stripes of flatterers, which within
Are lechery unto him, and so feed
His brutish sense with their afflicting sound,   415
As (dead to virtue) he permits himself
Be carried like a pitcher, by the ears,

413 *strokes, and stripes*. Blows, as aids to carnal pleasure.

To every act of vice: this is a case
Deserves our fear, and doth presage the nigh,
And close approach of blood and tyranny.   420
Flattery is midwife unto princes' rage:
And nothing sooner, doth help forth a tyrant,
Than that, and whisperers' grace, who have the time,
The place, the power, to make all men offenders.

ARRUNTIUS
He should be told this; and be bid dissemble   425
With fools, and blind men: we that know the evil,
Should hunt the palace-rats, or give them bane;
Fright hence these worse than ravens, that devour
The quick, where they but prey upon the dead:
He shall be told it.

SABINUS   Stay, Arruntius,   430
We must abide our opportunity:
And practise what is fit, as what is needful.
It is not safe t'enforce a sovereign's ear:
Princes hear well, if they at all will hear.

ARRUNTIUS
Ha? Say you so? well. In the meantime, Jove,   435
(Say not, but I do call upon thee now.)
Of all wild beasts, preserve me from a tyrant;
And of all tame, a flatterer.

SILIUS   'Tis well prayed.

TIBERIUS
Return the lords this voice, we are their creature:
And it is fit, a good, and honest prince,   440
Whom they, out of their bounty, have instructed
With so dilate, and absolute a power,
Should owe the office of it, to their service;
And good of all, and every citizen.
Nor shall it e'er repent us, to have wished   445
The Senate just, and favouring lords unto us,
Since their free loves do yield no less defence
T'a prince's state, than his own innocence.
Say then, there can be nothing in their thought
Shall want to please us, that hath pleasèd them;   450
Our suffrage rather shall prevent, than stay

433 *enforce* approach by force
441 *instructed* provided (Latin *instructum*)
442 *dilate* enlarged   445 *repent* make regret
451 *prevent* anticipate (Latin *prævenio*)

---

436 *Say not.* Don't bring up my former complaints against you.

Behind their wills: 'tis empire, to obey
Where such, so great, so grave, so good determine.
Yet, for the suit of Spain, t'erect a temple
In honour of our mother, and ourself,   455
We must (with pardon of the Senate) not
Assent thereto. Their lordships may object
Our not denying the same late request
Unto the Asian cities: we desire
That our defence, for suffering that, be known   460
In these brief reasons, with our after purpose.
Since deified Augustus hindered not
A temple to be built, at Pergamum,
In honour of himself, and sacred Rome,
We, that have all his deeds, and words observed   465
Ever, in place of laws, the rather followed
That pleasing precedent, because, with ours,
The Senate's reverence also, there, was joined.
But, as, t'have once received it, may deserve
The gain of pardon, so, to be adored   470
With the continued style, and note of gods,
Through all the provinces, were wild ambition,
And no less pride: yea, ev'n Augustus' name
Would early vanish, should it be profaned
With such promiscuous flatteries. For our part,   475
We here protest it, and are covetous
Posterity should know it, we are mortal;
And can but deeds of men: 'twere glory enough,
Could we be truly a prince. And, they shall add
Abounding grace, unto our memory,   480
That shall report us worthy our forefathers,
Careful of your affairs, constant in dangers,
And not afraid of any private frown
For public good. These things shall be to us
Temples, and statues, reared in your minds,   485
The fairest, and most during imagery:
For those of stone, or brass, if they become
Odious in judgement of posterity,
Are more contemned, as dying sepulchres,
Than ta'en for living monuments. We then   490
Make here our suit, alike to gods, and men,
The one, until the period of our race,
T'inspire us with a free, and quiet mind,
Discerning both divine, and human laws;

460 *suffering* allowing   471 *note* ceremony
478 *can* can do   492 *period of our race* end of our life

The other, to vouchsafe us after death,   495
An honourable mention, and fair praise,
T'accompany our actions, and our name:
The rest of greatness princes may command,
And (therefore) may neglect, only, a long,
A lasting, high, and happy memory   500
They should, without being satisfied, pursue.
Contempt of fame begets contempt of virtue.

NATTA
Rare!

SATRIUS Most divine!

SEJANUS   The oracles are ceased,
That only Cæsar, with their tongue, might speak.

ARRUNTIUS
Let me be gone, most felt, and open this!   505

CORDUS
Stay.

ARRUNTIUS What? to hear more cunning, and fine words,
With their sound flattered, ere their sense be meant?

TIBERIUS
Their choice of Antium, there to place the gift
Vowed to the goddess, for our mother's health,
We will the Senate know, we fairly like;   510
As also, of their grant to Lepidus,
For his repairing the Æmilian place,
And restoration of those monuments:
Their grace too in confining of Silanus,
To th'other isle Cithera, at the suit   515
Of his religious sister, much commends
Their policy, so tempered with their mercy.
But, for the honours, which they have decreed
To our Sejanus, to advance his statue
In Pompey's theatre (whose ruining fire   520
His vigilance, and labour kept restrained

505 *felt* easily perceived
511 *grant* permission
517 *policy* wisdom

---

503 A reference to Plutarch *On the Cessation of Oracles* and to the tradition
    that the oracles ceased upon the coming of Christ, because no one be-
    lieved in them.
509 Jonson explains in a marginal note, *Fortuna equestris*, a statue given by
    the Roman knights (at V, 179, 'Antium' for 'action' has been—probably
    wrongly—suggested because of the association).
512 The family court of the Æmilii, to whom Lepidus belonged. Perhaps
    'place' should be 'palace'.

In that one loss) they have, therein, outgone
Their own great wisdoms, by their skilful choice,
And placing of their bounties, on a man,
Whose merit more adorns the dignity,   525
Than that can him: and gives a benefit,
In taking, greater, than it can receive.
Blush not, Sejanus, thou great aid of Rome,
Associate of our labours, our chief helper,
Let us not force thy simple modesty   530
With offering at thy praise, for more we cannot,
Since there's no voice can take it. No man, here,
Receive our speeches, as hyperboles;
For we are far from flattering our friend,
(Let envy know) as from the need to flatter.   535
Nor let them ask the causes of our praise;
Princes have still their grounds reared with themselves,
Above the poor low flats of common men,
And, who will search the reasons of their acts,
Must stand on equal bases. Lead, away.   540
Our loves unto the Senate.
                    [*Exeunt* TIBERIUS, SEJANUS, *and retinue*]
ARRUNTIUS   Cæsar.
SABINUS   Peace.
CORDUS
Great Pompey's theatre was never ruined
Till now, that proud Sejanus hath a statue
Reared on his ashes.
ARRUNTIUS   Place the shame of soldiers,
Above the best of generals? crack the world!   545
And bruise the name of Romans into dust,
Ere we behold it!
SILIUS   Check your passion;
Lord Drusus tarries.
DRUSUS   Is my father mad?
Weary of life, and rule, lords? thus to heave
An idol up with praise! make him his mate!   550
His rival in the Empire!
ARRUNTIUS   O, good prince!

533 *hyperboles* exaggerations
551 *rival* partner

530f. *Let us . . . take it.* Don't let me do violence to your unfeigned modesty
    with attempting to praise you; more than attempt I cannot do, since no
    voice can adequately perform the task.
537f. *Princes have . . . common men.* Princes stand on a firmament suitably
    high, above the lower ground of the commonality.

DRUSUS

  Allow him statues? titles? honours? such,
  As he himself refuseth?

ARRUNTIUS   Brave, brave Drusus!

DRUSUS

  The first ascents to sovereignty are hard
  But, entered once, there never wants or means,   555
  Or ministers, to help th'aspirer on.

ARRUNTIUS

  True, gallant Drusus.

DRUSUS   We must shortly pray
  To modesty, that he will rest contented—

ARRUNTIUS

  Ay, where he is, and not write emperor.

SEJANUS, [LATIARIS,] etc.

He enters, followed with clients

SEJANUS

  There is your bill, and yours; bring you your man: 560
  I have moved for you, too, Latiaris.

DRUSUS   What?
  Is your vast greatness grown so blindly bold,
  That you will over us?

SEJANUS   Why, then give way.

DRUSUS

  Give way, Colossus? Do you lift? Advance you?
  Take that.

Drusus strikes him

ARRUNTIUS

          Good! brave! excellent brave Prince!   565

DRUSUS

  Nay, come, approach. What? stand you off? at gaze?
  It looks too full of death, for thy cold spirits.
  Avoid mine eye, dull camel, or my sword
  Shall make thy bravery fitter for a grave,
  Than for a triumph. I'll advance a statue,   570
  Of your own bulk; but 't shall be on the cross:
  Where I will nail your pride, at breadth, and length,
  And crack those sinews, which are yet but stretched
  With your swoll'n fortune's rage.

ARRUNTIUS   A noble prince!

561 *moved* interceded
563 *over* overmaster
564 *lift* rise (like a rearing horse)
566 *at gaze* in bewilderment (like a hunted animal)

ALL
> A Castor, a Castor, a Castor, a Castor!   575
> > *[Exeunt, leaving* SEJANUS]

SEJANUS
> He that, with such wrong moved, can bear it through
> With patience, and an even mind, knows how
> To turn it back. Wrath, covered, carries fate:
> Revenge is lost, if I profess my hate.
> What was my practice late, I'll now pursue   580
> As my fell justice. This hath styled it new.   *[Exit]*

CHORUS—OF MUSICIANS

Act II, [Scene i]

[Eudemus' garden. Enter] SEJANUS, LIVIA, EUDEMUS

SEJANUS
> Physician, thou art worthy of a province,
> For the great favours done unto our loves;
> And, but that greatest Livia bears a part
> In the requital of thy services,
> I should alone, despair of ought, like means,   5
> To give them worthy satisfaction.

LIVIA
> Eudemus, (I will see it) shall receive
> A fit, and full reward, for his large merit.
> But for this potion, we intend to Drusus,
> (No more our husband, now) whom shall we choose   10
> As the most apt, and abled instrument,
> To minister it to him?

EUDEMUS   I say, Lygdus.

SEJANUS
> Lygdus? what's he?

LIVIA   An eunuch Drusus loves.

EUDEMUS
> Ay, and his cup-bearer.

SEJANUS   Name not a second.
> If Drusus love him, and he have that place,   15
> We cannot think a fitter.

EUDEMUS   True, my lord,
> For free access, and trust, are two main aids.

---

5 *like* equal, adequate

SEJANUS
　Skilful physician!
LIVIA   But he must be wrought
　To th'undertaking, with some laboured art.
SEJANUS
　Is he ambitious?
LIVIA   No.
SEJANUS   Or covetous?   20
LIVIA
　Neither.
EUDEMUS   Yet, gold is a good general charm.
SEJANUS
　What is he then?
LIVIA   Faith, only wanton, light.
SEJANUS
　How! Is he young? and fair?
EUDEMUS   A delicate youth.
SEJANUS
　Send him to me, I'll work him. Royal lady,
　Though I have loved you long, and with that height   25
　Of zeal, and duty, (like the fire, which more
　It mounts, it trembles) thinking nought could add
　Unto the fervour, which your eye had kindled;
　Yet, now I see your wisdom, judgement, strength,
　Quickness, and will, to apprehend the means   30
　To your own good, and greatness, I protest
　Myself through rarefied, and turned all flame
　In your affection: such a spirit as yours,
　Was not created for the idle second
　To a poor flash, as Drusus; but to shine   35
　Bright, as the moon, among the lesser lights,
　And share the sovereignty of all the world.
　Then Livia triumphs in her proper sphere,
　When she, and her Sejanus shall divide
　The name of Cæsar; and Augusta's star   40
　Be dimmed with glory of a brighter beam:
　When Agrippina's fires are quite extinct,
　And the scarce-seen Tiberius borrows all
　His little light from us, whose folded arms
　Shall make one perfect orb. Who's that? Eudemus,   45
　Look, 'tis not Drusus? [*Exit* EUDEMUS] Lady, do not fear.
LIVIA
　Not I, my lord. My fear, and love of him
　Left me at once.

32 *through rarefied* entirely refined, purified

SEJANUS   Illustrous lady! stay—

[*Enter* EUDEMUS]

EUDEMUS
  I'll tell his lordship.
SEJANUS   Who is't, Eudemus?
EUDEMUS
  One of your lordship's servants, brings you word   50
  The Emperor hath sent for you.
SEJANUS   O! where is he?
  With your fair leave, dear Princess. I'll but ask
  A question, and return.
                 He goes out
EUDEMUS   Fortunate Princess!
  How you are blest in the fruition
  Of this unequalled man, this soul of Rome,   55
  The Empire's life, and voice of Cæsar's world!
LIVIA
  So blessed, my Eudemus, as to know
  The bliss I have, with what I ought to owe
  The means that wrought it. How do I look today?
EUDEMUS
  Excellent clear, believe it. This same fucus   60
  Was well laid on.
LIVIA   Me thinks, 'tis here not white.
EUDEMUS
  Lend me your scarlet, lady, 'Tis the sun
  Hath giv'n some little taint unto the ceruse,
  You should have used of the white oil I gave you.
  Sejanus, for your love! his very name   65
  Commandeth above Cupid, or his shafts —
(LIVIA
  Nay, now you've made it worse.
EUDEMUS   I'll help it straight.)
  And, but pronounced, is a sufficient charm
  Against all rumour; and of absolute power
  To satisfy for any lady's honour.   70
(LIVIA
  What do you now, Eudemus?
EUDEMUS   Make a light fucus,
  To touch you o'er withal.) Honoured Sejanus!
  What act (though ne'er so strange, and insolent)

48 *Illustrous* illustrious   54 *fruition* enjoyment (Latin *fruor*)
60 *fucus* cosmetic, face-wash
63 *ceruse* cosmetic of white lead

But that addition will at least bear out,
If't do not expiate?

LIVIA   Here, good physician.   75

EUDEMUS
I like this study to preserve the love
Of such a man, that comes not every hour
To greet the world. ('Tis now well, lady, you should
Use of the dentifrice, I prescribed you, too,
To clear your teeth, and the prepared pomatum,   80
To smooth the skin:) A lady cannot be
Too curious of her form, that still would hold
The heart of such a person, made her captive,
As you have his: who, to endear him more
In your clear eye, hath put away his wife,   85
The trouble of his bed, and your delights,
Fair Apicata, and made spacious room
To your new pleasures.

LIVIA   Have not we returned
That, with our hate of Drusus, and discovery
Of all his counsels?

EUDEMUS   Yes, and wisely, lady,   90
The ages that succeed, and stand far off
To gaze at your high prudence, shall admire
And reckon it an act, without your sex:
It hath that rare appearance. Some will think
Your fortune could not yield a deeper sound,   95
Than mixed with Drusus'; but, when they shall hear
That, and the thunder of Sejanus meet,
Sejanus, whose high name doth strike the stars,
And rings about the concave, great Sejanus,
Whose glories, style, and titles are himself,   100
The often iterating of Sejanus:
They then will lose their thoughts, and be ashamed
To take acquaintance of them.

                    [*Enter* SEJANUS]

SEJANUS   I must make
A rude departure, lady. Cæsar sends
With all his haste both of command, and prayer.   105
Be resolute in our plot; you have my soul,

74 *addition* title   82 *curious* careful (Latin *cura*)
93 *without* outside   95 *sound* sounding, measure of depth
104 *rude* early (Latin *rudis*)

88f. *Have not . . . his counsels?* Have not you and I justified Sejanus' actions
  in our favour by telling him Drusus' secrets?

As certain yours, as it is my body's.
And, wise physician, so prepare the poison
As you may lay the subtle operation
Upon some natural disease of his.   110
Your eunuch send to me. I kiss your hands,
Glory of ladies, and commend my love
To your best faith, and memory.

LIVIA   My lord,
I shall but change your words. Farewell. Yet, this
Remember for your heed, he loves you not;   115
You know, what I have told you: his designs
Are full of grudge, and danger: we must use
More than a common speed.

SEJANUS   Excellent lady,
How you do fire my blood!

LIVIA   Well, you must go?
The thoughts be best, are least set forth to show.   120

                                        [*Exit* SEJANUS]

EUDEMUS
When will you take some physic, lady?

LIVIA   When
I shall, Eudemus: but let Drusus' drug
Be first prepared.

EUDEMUS   Were Lygdus made, that's done;
I have it ready. And tomorrow morning,
I'll send you a perfume, first to resolve,   125
And procure sweat, and then prepare a bath
To cleanse, and clear the cutis; against when,
I'll have an excellent new fucus made,
Resistive 'gainst the sun, the rain, or wind,
Which you shall lay on with a breath, or oil,   130
As you best like, and last some fourteen hours.
This change came timely, lady, for your health;
And the restoring your complexion,
Which Drusus' choler had almost burnt up:
Wherein your fortune hath prescribed you better   135
Than art could do.

LIVIA   Thanks, good physician,
I'll use my fortune (you shall see) with reverence.
Is my coach ready?

EUDEMUS   It attends your highness.   [*Exeunt*]

109 *lay* blame, attribute
114 *change* exchange, repeat
123 *made* prepared
127 *cutis* skin

[Act II, Scene ii]

[An apartment in the palace. Enter] SEJANUS

SEJANUS
　If this be not revenge, when I have done
　And made it perfect, let Egyptian slaves,   140
　Parthians, and bare-foot Hebrews brand my face,
　And print my body full of injuries.
　Thou lost thyself, child Drusus, when thou thought's
　Thou could'st outskip my vengeance: or outstand
　The power I had to crush thee into air.   145
　Thy follies now shall taste what kind of man
　They have provoked, and this thy father's house
　Crack in the flame of my incensèd rage,
　Whose fury shall admit no shame, or mean.
　Adultery? it is the lightest ill,   150
　I will commit. A race of wicked acts
　Shall flow out of my anger, and o'erspread
　The world's wide face, which no posterity
　Shall e'er approve, nor yet keep silent: things,
　That for their cunning, close, and cruel mark,   155
　Thy father would wish his; and shall (perhaps)
　Carry the empty name, but we the prize.
　On then, my soul, and start not in thy course;
　Though heav'n drop sulphur, and hell belch out fire,
　Laugh at the idle terrors: tell proud Jove,   160
　Between his power, and thine, there is no odds.
　'Twas only fear, first, in the world made gods.

[Enter] TIBERIUS *[and retinue]*

TIBERIUS
　Is yet Sejanus come?
SEJANUS　　　　　　　　　　He's here, dread Cæsar.
TIBERIUS
　Let all depart that chamber, and the next: *[Exit retinue]*
　Sit down, my comfort. When the master-prince   165

143　*child* prince
144　*outstand* withstand
148　*incensèd* kindled (Latin *incendo*)
158　*start* leap aside

140f. *Egyptian . . . Hebrews.* Races which gave homage to Rome, and thus
　humiliating for a Roman to be wounded by.

Of all the world, Sejanus, saith, he fears;
Is it not fatal?
SEJANUS   Yes, to those are feared.
TIBERIUS
And not to him?
SEJANUS   Not, if he wisely turn
That part of fate he holdeth, first on them.
TIBERIUS
That nature, blood, and laws of kind forbid.   170
SEJANUS
Do policy, and state forbid it?
TIBERIUS   No.
SEJANUS
The rest of poor respects, then, let go by:
State is enough to make th'act just, them guilty.
TIBERIUS
Long hate pursues such acts.
SEJANUS   Whom hatred frights,
Let him not dream on sovereignty.
TIBERIUS   Are rites   175
Of faith, love, piety, to be trod down?
Forgotten? and made vain?
SEJANUS   All for a crown.
The prince, who shames a tyrant's name to bear,
Shall never dare do anything, but fear;
All the command of sceptres quite doth perish   180
If it begin religious thoughts to cherish:
Whole empires fall, swayed by those nice respects.
It is the licence of dark deeds protects
Ev'n states most hated: when no laws resist
The sword, but that it acteth what it list.   185
TIBERIUS
Yet so, we may do all things cruelly,
Not safely:
SEJANUS   Yes, and do them thoroughly.
TIBERIUS
Knows yet, Sejanus, whom we point at?
SEJANUS   Ay,
Or else my thought, my sense, or both do err:
'Tis Agrippina?
TIBERIUS   She; and her proud race.   190

171 *state* statecraft
172 *respects* scruples

188 *Ay* might be emended *sir* to preserve the rhyme.

SEJANUS
    Proud? dangerous, Cæsar. For in them apace
    The father's spirit shoots up. Germanicus
    Lives in their looks, their gait, their form, t'upbraid us
    With his close death, if not revenge the same.
TIBERIUS
    The act's not known.
SEJANUS   Not proved. But whispering fame   195
    Knowledge, and proof doth to the jealous give,
    Who, than to fail, would their own thought believe.
    It is not safe, the children draw long breath,
    That are provokèd by a parent's death.
TIBERIUS
    It is as dangerous, to make them hence,   200
    If nothing but their birth be their offence.
SEJANUS
    Stay, till they strike at Cæsar: then their crime
    Will be enough, but late, and out of time
    For him to punish.
TIBERIUS   Do they purpose it?
SEJANUS
    You know, sir, thunder speaks not till it hit.   205
    Be not secure: none swiftlier are oppressed,
    Than they, whom confidence betrays to rest.
    Let not your daring make your danger such:
    All power's to be feared, where 'tis too much.
    The youths are (of themselves) hot, violent,   210
    Full of great thought; and that male-spirited dame,
    Their mother, slacks no means to put them on,
    By large allowance, popular presentings,
    Increase of train, and state, suing for titles,
    Hath them commended with like prayers, like vows,   215
    To the same gods, with Cæsar: days and nights
    She spends in banquets, and ambitious feasts
    For the nobility; where Caius Silius,
    Titius Sabinus, old Arruntius,
    Asinius Gallus, Furnius, Regulus,   220
    And others, of that discontented list,
    Are the prime guests. There, and to these, she tells
    Whose niece she was, whose daughter, and whose wife,
    And then must they compare her with Augusta,

194 *close* secret   195 *fame* rumour (Latin *fama*)
197 *than to fail* rather than do without proof   212 *slacks* spares
213 *large allowance* 'free rein'
223 *niece* granddaughter (Latin *neptis*)

Ay, and prefer her too, commend her form,   225
Extol her fruitfulness; at which a show'r
Falls for the memory of Germanicus,
Which they blow over straight, with windy praise,
And puffing hopes of her aspiring sons:
Who, with these hourly ticklings, grow so pleased,   230
And wantonly conceited of themselves,
As now, they stick not to believe they're such,
As these do give 'em out: and would be thought
(More than competitors) immediate heirs.
Whilst to their thirst of rule they win the rout   235
(That's still the friend of novelty) with hope
Of future freedom, which on every change,
That greedily, though emptily, expects.
Cæsar, 'tis age in all things breeds neglects,
And princes that will keep old dignity,   240
Must not admit too youthful heirs stand by;
Not their own issue: but so darkly set
As shadows are in picture, to give height,
And lustre to themselves.
TIBERIUS   We will command
    Their rank thoughts down, and with a stricter hand   245
    Than we have yet put forth, their trains must bate,
    Their titles, feasts and factions.
SEJANUS   Or your state.
    But how sir, will you work?
TIBERIUS   Confine 'em,
SEJANUS   No.
    They are too great, and that too faint a blow,
    To give them now: it would have served at first,   250
    When, with the weakest touch, their knot had burst.
    But, now, your care must be, not to detect
    The smallest cord, or line of your suspect,
    For such, who know the weight of princes' fear,
    Will, when they find themselves discovered, rear   255
    Their forces, like seen snakes, that else would lie
    Rolled in their circles, close: nought is more high,
    Daring, or desperate, than offenders found;
    Where guilt is, rage, and courage both abound.
    The course must be, to let 'em still swell up,   260
    Riot, and surfeit on blind Fortune's cup;
    Give 'em more place, more dignities, more style,

246 *trains* ruses (frequent)   *bate* abate
252 *detect* reveal   253 *suspect* suspicion
259 *both* Q (F doth)

Call 'em to court, to Senate: in the while,
Take from their strength some one or twain, or more
Of the main fautors; (it will fright the store)   265
And, by some by-occasion. Thus, with slight
You shall disarm them first, and they (in night
Of their ambition) not perceive the train,
Till, in the engine, they are caught, and slain.

TIBERIUS
We would not kill, if we knew how to save;   270
Yet, than a throne, 'tis cheaper give a grave.
Is there no way to bind them by deserts?

SEJANUS
Sir, wolves do change their hair, but not their hearts.
While thus your thought unto a mean is tied,
You neither dare enough, nor do provide.   275
All modesty is fond; and chiefly where
The subject is no less compelled to bear,
Than praise his sovereign's acts.

TIBERIUS   We can no longer
Keep on our mask to thee, our dear Sejanus;
Thy thoughts are ours, in all, and we but proved   280
Their voice, in our designs, which by assenting
Hath more confirmed us, than if heartening Jove
Had, from his hundred statues, bid us strike,
And at the stroke clicked all his marble thumbs.
But, who shall first be struck?

SEJANUS   First, Caius Silius;   285
He is the most of mark, and most of danger:
In power, and reputation equal strong,
Having commanded an imperial army
Seven years together, vanquished Sacrovir
In Germany, and thence obtained to wear   290
The ornaments triumphal. His steep fall,
By how much it doth give the weightier crack,

265 *fautors* supporters   *store* largest part, remainder
266 *by-occasion* incidental opportunity   267 *them* Q (F *omits*)
272 *bind them by deserts* gain their loyalty by favours
275 *provide* use foresight (Latin *provideo*)
276 *modesty* holding to a middle way
      fond foolish
280 *proved* tested   292 *crack* sound

---

284 *clicked all his marble thumbs.* Gave the gesture that meant a defeated
      gladiator was to be condemned; approved the sentence of death.
291 *ornaments triumphal.* Devices and garments worn by victorious generals,
      in place of the traditional triumph or procession through Rome, at this
      time reserved to the royal family.

R—C

Will send more wounding terror to the rest,
Command them stand aloof, and give more way
To our surprising of the principal.   295

TIBERIUS
But what, Sabinus?

SEJANUS   Let him grow awhile,
His fate is not yet ripe: we must not pluck
At all together, lest we catch ourselves.
And there's Arruntius too, he only talks.
But Sosia, Silius' wife, would be wound in   300
Now, for she hath a fury in her breast
More, than hell ever knew; and would be sent
Thither in time. Then, is there one Cremutius
Cordus, a writing fellow, they have got
To gather notes of the precedent times,   305
And make them into annals; a most tart
And bitter spirit (I hear) who, under colour
Of praising those, doth tax the present state,
Censures the men, the actions, leaves no trick,
No practice unexamined, parallels   310
The times, the governments, a professed champion,
For the old liberty—

TIBERIUS   A perishing wretch.
As if there were that chaos bred in things,
That laws, and liberty would not rather choose
To be quite broken, and ta'en hence by us,   315
Than have the stain to be preserved by such.
Have we the means, to make these guilty, first?

SEJANUS
Trust that to me: let Cæsar, by his power,
But cause a formal meeting of the Senate,
I will have matter, and accusers ready.   320

TIBERIUS
But how? let us consult.

SEJANUS   We shall misspend
The time of action. Counsels are unfit
In business, where all rest is more pernicious
Than rashness can be. Acts of this close kind
Thrive more by execution, than advice.   325
There is no lingering in that work begun,
Which cannot praisèd be, until through done.

TIBERIUS
Our edict shall, forthwith, command a court.

300 *wound in* ensnared

While I can live, I will prevent earth's fury:
Ἐμοῦ θανόντος γαῖα μιχθήτω πυρί.　　　　　　　　　[*Exit*]　330

[*Enter*] POSTHUMUS

POSTHUMUS
　My lord Sejanus—
SEJANUS　　　　　　Julius Posthumus,
　Come with my wish! what news from Agrippina's?
POSTHUMUS
　Faith none. They all lock up themselves a' late;
　Or talk in character: I have not seen
　A company so changed. Except they had　　　　　335
　Intelligence by augury of our practice.
SEJANUS
　When were you there?
POSTHUMUS　　　　　Last night.
SEJANUS　　　　　　　　And what guests found you?
POSTHUMUS
　Sabinus, Silius, (the old list,) Arruntius,
　Furnius, and Gallus.
SEJANUS　　　　　Would not these talk?
POSTHUMUS　　　　　　　　　Little.
　And yet we offered choice of argument.　　　　340
　Satrius was with me.
SEJANUS　　　　　Well: 'tis guilt enough
　Their often meeting. You forgot t'extol
　The hospitable lady?
POSTHUMUS　　　　No, that trick
　Was well put home, and had succeeded too,
　But that Sabinus caught a caution out;　　　　345
　For she began to swell:
SEJANUS　　　　　And may she burst.
　Julius, I would have you go instantly,
　Unto the palace of the great Augusta,
　And, (by your kindest friend,) get swift access;
　Acquaint her, with these meetings: tell the words　　350
　You brought me, (th'other day) of Silius,
　Add somewhat to 'em. Make her understand
　The danger of Sabinus, and the times,

334 *character* secret code　　340 *argument* topic
345 *caught a caution out* gave warning

330 Translated by Milton, *Reason of Church Government*, I, v, 'When I die,
　　let the earth be rolled in flames'. The Greek was a favourite phrase of
　　Tiberius, from a lost source.
349 *kindest friend*. Jonson's marginal note explains, *Mutilia Prisca*.

Out of his closeness. Give Arruntius words
Of malice against Cæsar; so, to Gallus: 355
But (above all) to Agrippina. Say,
(As you may truly) that her infinite pride,
Propped with the hopes of her too fruitful womb,
With popular studies gapes for sovereignty;
And threatens Cæsar. Pray Augusta then,   360
That for her own, great Cæsar's, and the pub-
Lic safety, she be pleased to urge these dangers.
Cæsar is too secure (he must be told,
And best he'll take it from a mother's tongue.)
Alas! what is't for us to sound, t'explore,   365
To watch, oppose, plot, practise, or prevent,
If he, for whom it is so strongly laboured,
Shall, out of greatness, and free spirit, be
Supinely negligent? Our city's now
Divided as in time o'th' civil war,   370
And men forbear not to declare themselves
Of Agrippina's party. Every day,
The faction multiplies; and will do more
If not resisted: you can best enlarge it
As you find audience. Noble Posthumus,   375
Commend me to your Prisca: and pray her,
She will solicit this great business
To earnest, and most present execution,
With all her utmost credit with Augusta.
POSTHUMUS
    I shall not fail in my instructions.   [*Exit*]   380
SEJANUS
    This second (from his mother) will well urge
Our late design, and spur on Cæsar's rage:
Which else might grow remiss. The way, to put
A prince in blood, is to present the shapes
Of dangers, greater than they are (like late,   385
Or early shadows) and, sometimes, to feign
Where there are none, only, to make him fear;

354 *Give* attribute to
359 *studies* support (Latin *popularibus studiis*)
    gapes for covets

---

361 *pub-/Lic.* Herford and Simpson cite parallels for this 'ugly enjambment'
    from Jonson and his contemporaries; but the device is actually an overt
    classicism (*synapheia*), and appropriate references should include, e.g.,
    Horace, *Odes* I, 2, 18–19; I, 25, 11–12; II, 16, 7–8, and Catullus, 11,
    11–12; 61, 82–83.
374f. *you can best . . . find audience.* You can best embroider the story accord-
    ing to your audience.

His fear will make him cruel: and once entered,
He doth not easily learn to stop, or spare
Where he may doubt. This have I made my rule,   390
To thrust Tiberius into tyranny,
And make him toil, to turn aside those blocks,
Which I alone, could not remove with safety.
Drusus once gone, Germanicus' three sons
Would clog my way; whose guards have too much faith   395
To be corrupted: and their mother known
Of too too unreproved a chastity,
To be attempted, as light Livia was.
Work then, my art, on Cæsar's fears, as they
On those they fear, till all my lets be cleared: 400
And he in ruins of his house, and hate
Of all his subjects, bury his own state:
When, with my peace, and safety, I will rise,
By making him the public sacrifice.   [*Exit*]

[Act II, Scene iii]

[Agrippina's house. Enter] SATRIUS, NATTA

SATRIUS
They're grown exceeding circumspect, and wary.   405
NATTA
They have us in the wind: and yet, Arruntius
Cannot contain himself.
SATRIUS   Tut, he's not yet
Looked after, there are others more desired,
That are more silent.
NATTA   Here he comes. Away.   [*Exeunt*]

[Enter] SABINUS, ARRUNTIUS, CORDUS

SABINUS
How is it, that these beagles haunt the house   410
Of Agrippina?
ARRUNTIUS   O, they hunt, they hunt.
There is some game here lodged, which they must rouse,
To make the great one's sport.
CORDUS   Did you observe
How they inveighed 'gainst Cæsar?
ARRUNTIUS   Ay, baits, baits,
For us to bite at: would I have my flesh   415

400 *lets* Q (F betts)
408 *Looked after* sought for

Torn by the public hook, these qualified hang-men
Should be my company.
CORDUS   Here comes another.
                    [AFER *passeth by*]
ARRUNTIUS
Ay, there's a man, Afer the orator!
One, that hath phrases, figures, and fine flowers,
To strew his rhetoric with, and doth make haste   420
To get him note, or name, by any offer
Where blood, or gain be objects; steeps his words,
When he would kill, in artificial tears:
The crocodile of Tiber! him I love,
That man is mine. He hath my heart, and voice,   425
When I would curse, he, he.
SABINUS   Contemn the slaves,
Their present lives will be their future graves.   [*Exeunt*]

        [*Enter*] SILIUS, AGRIPPINA, NERO, SOSIA

SILIUS
May't please your highness not forget yourself,
I dare not, with my manners, to attempt
Your trouble farther.
AGRIPPINA   Farewell, noble Silius.   430
SILIUS
Most royal Princess.
AGRIPPINA   Sosia stays with us?
SILIUS
She is your servant, and doth owe your grace
An honest, but unprofitable love.
AGRIPPINA
How can that be, when there's no gain, but virtue's?
SILIUS
You take the moral, not the politic sense.   435
I meant, as she is bold, and free of speech,
Earnest to utter what her zealous thought
Travails withal, in honour of your house;
Which act, as it is simply born in her,
Partakes of love, and honesty, but may,   440
By th'over-often, and unseasoned use,
Turn to your loss, and danger: for your state

419 *figures . . . flowers* turns of rhetorical speech
429 *manners* usual behaviour   *attempt* vex with afflictions
434 *virtue's* Q (F vertuous)

---

416 *public hook.* Executed criminals were dragged to the Gemonies by the
    executioner's hook, and thence three days after to the Tiber.

Is waited on by envies, as by eyes;
And every second guest your tables take,
Is a fee'd spy, t'observe who goes, who comes,   445
What conference you have, with whom, where, when,
What the discourse is, what the looks, the thoughts
Of every person there, they do extract,
And make into a substance.
AGRIPPINA   Hear me, Silius,
Were all Tiberius' body stuck with eyes,   450
And every wall, and hanging in my house
Transparent, as this lawn I wear, or air;
Yea, had Sejanus both his ears as long
As to my inmost closet: I would hate
To whisper any thought, or change an act,   455
To be made Juno's rival. Virtue's forces
Show ever noblest in conspicuous courses.
SILIUS
'Tis great, and bravely spoken, like the spirit
Of Agrippina: yet, your highness knows,
There is nor loss, nor shame in providence: 460
Few can, what all should do, beware enough.
You may perceive with what officious face,
Satrius, and Natta, Afer, and the rest
Visit your house, of late, t'enquire the secrets;
And with what bold, and privileged art, they rail   465
Against Augusta: yea, and at Tiberius,
Tell tricks of Livia, and Sejanus, all
T'excite, and call your indignation on,
That they might hear it at more liberty.
AGRIPPINA
You're too suspicious, Silius.
SILIUS   Pray the gods,   470
I be so Agrippina: but I fear
Some subtle practice. They, that durst to strike
At so exampless, and unblamed a life,
As, that of the renowned Germanicus,
Will not sit down, with that exploit alone: 475
He threatens many, that hath injured one.
NERO
'Twere best rip forth their tongues, sear out their eyes,
When next they come.
SOSIA   A fit reward for spies.
                [Enter] DRUSUS JUNIOR

449 AGRIPPINA edd. (Q, F ARR.)   460 *providence* careful foresight

DRUSUS JUNIOR
  Hear you the rumour?
AGRIPPINA   `What?
DRUSUS JUNIOR   Drusus is dying.
AGRIPPINA
  Dying?
NERO   That's strange!
AGRIPPINA   You were with him, yesternight.   480
DRUSUS JUNIOR
  One met Eudemus, the physician,
  Sent for, but now: who thinks he cannot live.
SILIUS
  Thinks? if't be arrived at that, he knows,
  Or none.
AGRIPPINA   This's quick! what should be his disease?
SILIUS
  Poison. Poison—
AGRIPPINA   How, Silius!
NERO   What's that?   485
SILIUS
  Nay, nothing. There was (late) a certain blow
  Giv'n on the face.
NERO   Ay, to Sejanus?
SILIUS   True.
DRUSUS JUNIOR
  And, what of that?
SILIUS   I'm glad I gave it not.
NERO
  But, there is somewhat else?
SILIUS   Yes, private meetings,
  With a great lady, at a physician's,   490
  And, a wife turned away—
NERO   Ha!
SILIUS   Toys, mere toys:
  What wisdom's now i'th' streets? i'th' common mouth?
DRUSUS JUNIOR
  Fears, whisperings, tumults, noise, I know not what:
  They say, the Senate sit.
SILIUS   I'll thither, straight;
  And see what's in the forge.
AGRIPPINA   Good Silius do.   495
  Sosia, and I will in.

479 *rumour* popular report
480 *You were* one syllable (F yo' were)
484 *should be* is said to be

SILIUS   Haste you, my lords,
To visit the sick Prince: tender your loves,
And sorrows to the people. This Sejanus
(Trust my divining soul) hath plots on all:
No tree, that stops his prospect, but must fall. *[Exeunt]*   500

CHORUS—OF MUSICIANS

[Act III, Scene i]

The Senate. [Enter] SEJANUS, VARRO, LATIARIS. COTTA,
AFER. [SABINUS] GALLUS, LEPIDUS, ARRUNTIUS.
PRÆCONES, LICTORES

SEJANUS
'Tis only you must urge against him, Varro,
Nor I, nor Cæsar may appear therein,
Except in your defence, who are the Consul:
And, under colour of late enmity
Between your father, and his, may better do it,   5
As free from all suspicion of a practice.
Here be your notes, what points to touch at; read:
Be cunning in them. Afer has them too.
VARRO
But he is summoned?
SEJANUS   No. It was debated
By Cæsar, and concluded as most fit   10
To take him unprepared.
AFER   And prosecute
All under name of treason.
VARRO   I conceive.
SABINUS
Drusus being dead, Cæsar will not be here.
GALLUS
What should the business of this Senate be?
ARRUNTIUS
That can my subtle whisperers tell you: we,   15
That are the good-dull-noble lookers on,

500 *prospect* view (Latin *prospectus*), with a pun on 'future oppor-
      tunities'
s.d. SABINUS edd. (F *omits*)
 11 *take him* Q (F him take)

---

  5 *and his*. Should be *and him*, for Silius superseded Varro's father in the
    war against Sacrovir. In the Roman view, this personal element would
    have guaranteed Varro's sincerity.

Are only called to keep the marble warm.
What should we do with those deep mysteries,
Proper to these fine heads? let them alone.
Our ignorance may, perchance, help us be saved   20
From whips, and furies.
GALLUS   See, see, see, their action!
ARRUNTIUS
Ay, now their heads do travail, now they work;
Their faces run like shuttles, they are weaving
Some curious cobweb to catch flies.
SABINUS   Observe,
They take their places.
ARRUNTIUS   What so low?
GALLUS   O yes,   25
They must be seen to flatter Cæsar's grief
Though but in sitting.
VARRO   Bid us silence.
PRÆCO   Silence.
VARRO
Fathers Conscript, may this our present meeting
Turn fair, and fortunate to the Commonwealth.

          [Enter] SILIUS, SENATE

SEJANUS
See, Silius enters.
SILIUS   Hail grave Fathers.
LICTOR   Stand.   30
Silius, forbear thy place.
SENATORS   How!
PRÆCO   Silius stand forth,
The Consul hath to charge thee.
LICTOR   Room for Cæsar.
ARRUNTIUS
Is he come too? nay then expect a trick.
SABINUS
Silius accused? sure he will answer nobly.

          [Enter] TIBERIUS, *[etc.]*

TIBERIUS
We stand amazed, Fathers, to behold   35
This general dejection. Wherefore sit
Rome's Consuls thus dissolved, as they had lost

30 SEJANUS Q (F *omits*)
    Stand stay where you are
37 *dissolved* neglectful (Latin *dissolutus*)

All the remembrance both of style, and place?
It not becomes. No woes are of fit weight,
To make the honour of the Empire stoop: 40
Though I, in my peculiar self, may meet
Just reprehension, that so suddenly,
And, in so fresh a grief, would greet the Senate,
When private tongues, of kinsmen, and allies,
(Inspired with comforts) loathly are endured,   45
The face of men not seen, and scarce the day,
To thousands, that communicate our loss.
Nor can I argue these of weakness; since
They take but natural ways: yet I must seek
For stronger aids, and those fair helps draw out   50
From warm embraces of the Commonwealth.
Our mother, great Augusta, is struck with time,
Ourself impressed with agèd characters,
Drusus is gone, his children young, and babes,
Our aims must now reflect on those, that may   55
Give timely succour to these present ills,
And are our only glad-surviving hopes,
The noble issue of Germanicus,
Nero, and Drusus: might it please the Consul
Honour them in, (they both attend without.)   60
I would present them to the Senate's care,
And raise those suns of joy, that should drink up
These floods of sorrow, in your drownèd eyes.

ARRUNTIUS

By Jove, I am not Œdipus enough,
To understand this Sphinx.

SABINUS   The Princes come.   65

        [*Enter*] NERO, DRUSUS JUNIOR

TIBERIUS

Approach you noble Nero, noble Drusus,
These Princes, Fathers, when their parent died,
I gave unto their uncle, with this prayer,
That, though he'd proper issue of his own,
He would no less bring up, and foster these,   70
Than that self-blood; and by that act confirm
Their worths to him, and to posterity:
Drusus ta'en hence, I turn my prayers to you,
And, 'fore our country, and our gods, beseech

41 *peculiar* private (frequent)
47 *communicate* share (Latin *communico*)
68 *uncle* Drusus senior (not strictly their uncle)

You take, and rule Augustus' nephew's sons,   75
Sprung of the noblest ancestors; and so
Accomplish both my duty, and your own.
Nero, and Drusus, these shall be to you
In place of parents, these your fathers, these,
And not unfitly: for you are so born,   80
As all your good, or ill's the Commonwealth's.
Receive them, you strong guardians; and blest gods,
Make all their actions answer to their bloods:
Let their great titles find increase by them,   ,
Not they by titles. Set them, as in place,   85
So in example, above all the Romans:
And may they know no rivals, but themselves.
Let Fortune give them nothing; but attend
Upon their virtue: and that still come forth
Greater than hope, and better than their fame.   90
Relieve me, Fathers, with your general voice.

SENATORS
May all the gods consent to Cæsar's wish,
And add to any honours, that may crown
The hopeful issue of Germanicus.

TIBERIUS
We thank you, reverend Fathers, in their right.   95

ARRUNTIUS
If this were true now! but the space, the space
Between the breast, and lips—Tiberius' heart
Lies a thought farther, than another man's.

TIBERIUS
My comforts are so flowing in my joys,
As, in them, all my streams of grief are lost,   100
No less than are land-waters in the sea,
Or showers in rivers; though their cause was such,
As might have sprinkled ev'n the gods with tears:
Yet since the greater doth embrace the less,
We covetously obey.

(ARRUNTIUS   Well acted, Cæsar.)   105

TIBERIUS
And, now I am the happy witness made
Of your so much desired affections,
To this great issue, I could wish, the fates
Would here set peaceful period to my days;

105 *covetously* eagerly

---

93 Jonson adds in the margin, *A form of speaking they had,* and after III,
142, *Another form.*

    However, to my labours, I entreat   110
    (And beg it of this Senate) some fit ease.
(ARRUNTIUS
    Laugh, Fathers, laugh: have you no spleens about you?)
TIBERIUS
    The burden is too heavy, I sustain
    On my unwilling shoulders; and I pray
    It may be taken off, and reconferred   115
    Upon the Consuls, or some other Roman,
    More able, and more worthy.
(ARRUNTIUS   Laugh on, still.)
SABINUS
    Why, this doth render all the rest suspected!
GALLUS
    It poisons all.
ARRUNTIUS   O, do you taste it then?
SABINUS
    It takes away my faith to any thing   120
    He shall hereafter speak.
ARRUNTIUS   Ay, to pray that,
    Which would be to his head as hot as thunder,
    ('Gainst which he wears that charm) should but the court
    Receive him at his word.
GALLUS   Hear.
TIBERIUS   For myself,
    I know my weakness, and so little covet   125
    (Like some gone past) the weight that will oppress me,
    As my ambition is the counter-point.
(ARRUNTIUS
    Finely maintained; good still.)
SEJANUS   But Rome, whose blood,
    Whose nerves, whose life, whose very frame relies
    On Cæsar's strength, no less than heav'n on Atlas,   130
    Cannot admit it but with general ruin.
(ARRUNTIUS
    Ah! are you there, to bring him off?)
SEJANUS   Let Cæsar
    No more than urge a point so contrary
    To Cæsar's greatness, the grieved Senate's vows,
    Or Rome's necessity.
(GALLUS   He comes about.   135

112 *spleens* thought to be the seat of laughter
127 *counter-point* opposite   132 *bring him off* aid him

---

123 Jonson adds in the margin, *A wreath of laurel.*

ARRUNTIUS
   More nimbly than Vertumnus.)
TIBERIUS   For the public,
   I may be drawn, to show, I can neglect
   All private aims; though I affect my rest:
   But, if the Senate still command me serve,
   I must be glad to practise my obedience.   140
(ARRUNTIUS
   You must, and will, sir. We do know it.)
SENATORS   Cæsar,
   Live long, and happy, great, and royal Cæsar,
   The gods preserve thee, and thy modesty,
   Thy wisdom, and thy innocence.
(ARRUNTIUS   Where is't?
   The prayer's made before the subject.)
SENATORS   Guard   145
   His meekness, Jove, his piety, his care,
   His bounty—
ARRUNTIUS   And his subtlety, I'll put in:
   Yet he'll keep that himself, without the gods.
   All prayers are vain for him.
TIBERIUS   We will not hold
   Your patience, Fathers, with long answer; but   150
   Shall still contend to be, what you desire,
   And work to satisfy so great a hope:
   Proceed to your affairs.
ARRUNTIUS   Now, Silius, guard thee;
   The curtain's drawing. Afer advanceth.
PRÆCO   Silence.
AFER
   Cite Caius Silius.
PRÆCO   Caius Silius.
SILIUS   Here.   155
AFER
   The triumph that thou hadst in Germany
   For thy late victory on Sacrovir,
   Thou hast enjoyed so freely, Caius Silius,
   As no man it envied thee; nor would Cæsar,
   Or Rome admit, that thou wert then defrauded   160
   Of any honours, thy deserts could claim,
   In the fair service of the Commonwealth:
   But now, if, after all their loves, and graces,

160 *admit* allow, permit

(Thy actions, and their courses being discovered)
It shall appear to Cæsar, and this Senate,   165
Thou hast defiled those glories, with thy crimes—

SILIUS
Crimes?

AFER   Patience, Silius.

SILIUS   Tell thy mule of patience,
I am a Roman. What are my crimes? Proclaim them.
Am I too rich? too honest for the times?
Have I or treasure, jewels, land, or houses   170
That some informer gapes for? Is my strength
Too much to be admitted? Or my knowledge?
These now are crimes.

AFER   Nay, Silius, if the name
Of crime so touch thee, with what impotence
Wilt thou endure the matter to be searched?   175

SILIUS
I tell thee, Afer, with more scorn, than fear:
Employ your mercenary tongue, and art.
Where's my accuser?

VARRO   Here.

ARRUNTIUS   Varro? The Consul?
Is he thrust in?

VARRO   'Tis I accuse thee, Silius.
Against the majesty of Rome, and Cæsar,   180
I do pronounce thee here a guilty cause,
First, of beginning, and occasioning,
Next, drawing out the war in Gallia,
For which thou late triumph'st; dissembling long
That Sacrovir to be an enemy,   185
Only to make thy entertainment more,
Whilst thou, and thy wife Sosia polled the province;
Wherein, with sordid-base desire of gain,
Thou hast discredited thy actions' worth
And been a traitor to the state.

SILIUS   Thou liest.   190

ARRUNTIUS
I thank thee, Silius, speak so still, and often.

VARRO
If I not prove it, Cæsar, but injustly
Have called him into trial, here I bind

174 *impotence* lack of self-restraint
181 *pronounce . . . cause* declare . . . agent
186 *entertainment* employment
187 *polled* plundered

    Myself to suffer, what I claim 'gainst him;
    And yield, to have what I have spoke, confirmed   195
    By judgement of the court, and all good men.
SILIUS
    Cæsar, I crave to have my cause deferred,
    Till this man's consulship be out.
TIBERIUS   We cannot,
    Nor may we grant it.
SILIUS   Why? shall he design
    My day of trial? is he my accuser?   200
    And must he be my judge?
TIBERIUS   It hath been usual,
    And is a right, that custom hath allowed
    The magistrate, to call forth private men;
    And to appoint their day: which privilege
    We may not in the Consul see infringed,   205
    By whose deep watches, and industrious care
    It is so laboured, as the Commonwealth
    Receive no loss, by any oblique course.
SILIUS
    Cæsar, thy fraud is worse than violence.
TIBERIUS
    Silius, mistake us not, we dare not use   210
    The credit of the Consul, to thy wrong,
    But only do preserve his place, and power,
    So far as it concerns the dignity,
    And honour of the state.
ARRUNTIUS   Believe him, Silius.
COTTA
    Why, so he may, Arruntius.
ARRUNTIUS   I say so.   215
    And he may choose to.
TIBERIUS   By the Capitol,
    And all our gods, but that the dear Republic,
    Our sacred laws, and just authority
    Are interest'd therein, I should be silent.
AFER
    Please Cæsar to give way unto his trial.   220
    He shall have justice.

199f. (204) *design* (*appoint*) *day* prosecute (Latin *diem dico*)
207 *laboured* accomplished with labour
219 *interest'd* have a stake in

---

216 *choose to.* Q, F, cdd. *too*, perhaps the correct reading, although Jonson
    does spell the particle *too* as well; cf. IV, 46, for a similar problem.

SILIUS   Nay, I shall have law;
　Shall I not Afer? speak.
AFER   Would you have more?
SILIUS
　No, my well-spoken man, I would no more;
　Nor less: might I enjoy it natural,
　Not taught to speak unto your present ends,   225
　Free from thine, his, and all your unkind handling,
　Furious enforcing, most unjust presuming,
　Malicious, and manifold applying,
　Foul wresting, and impossible construction.
AFER
　He raves, he raves.
SILIUS   Thou durst not tell me so,   230
　Had'st thou not Cæsar's warrant. I can see
　Whose power condemns me.
VARRO   This betrays his spirit.
　This doth enough declare him what he is.
SILIUS
　What am I? speak.
VARRO   An enemy to the State.
SILIUS
　Because I am an enemy to thee,   235
　And such corrupted ministers of the State,
　That here art made a present instrument
　To gratify it with thine own disgrace.
SEJANUS
　This, to the Consul, is most insolent!
　And impious!
SILIUS   Ay, take part. Reveal yourselves.   240
　Alas, I scent not your confederacies?
　Your plots, and combinations? I not know
　Minion Sejanus hates me; and that all
　This boast of law, and law, is but a form,
　A net of Vulcan's filing, a mere engine,   245
　To take that life by a pretext of justice,
　Which you pursue in malice? I want brain,
　Or nostril to persuade me, that your ends,
　And purposes are made to what they are,
　Before my answer? O, you equal gods,   250
　Whose justice not a world of wolf-turned men
　Shall make me to accuse (how e'er provoke)

222 *more?* edd. (F mo)
229 *construction* interpretation of the law   245 *filing* workmanship
250 *equal* impartial   252 *provoke* provoked

Have I for this so oft engaged myself?
Stood in the heat, and fervour of a fight,
When Phœbus sooner hath forsook the day   255
Than I the field? Against the blue-eyed Gauls?
And crispèd Germans? when our Roman eagles
Have fanned the fire, with their labouring wings,
And no blow dealt, that left not death behind it?
When I have charged, alone, into the troops   260
Of curled Sicambrians, routed them, and came
Not off, with backward ensigns of a slave,
But forward marks, wounds on my breast, and face,
Were meant to thee, O Cæsar, and thy Rome?
And have I this return? did I, for this,   265
Perform so noble, and so brave defeat,
On Sacrovir? (O Jove, let it become me
To boast my deeds, when he, whom they concern,
Shall thus forget them.)
AFER   Silius, Silius,
These are the common customs of thy blood,   270
When it is high with wine, as now with rage:
This well agrees, with that intemperate vaunt,
Thou lately made'st at Agrippina's table,
That when all other of the troops were prone
To fall into rebellion, only yours   275
Remained in their obedience. You were he, ·
That saved the Empire; which had then been lost,
Had but your legions, there, rebelled, or mutined.
Your virtue met, and fronted every peril.
You gave to Cæsar, and to Rome their surety.   280
Their name, their strength, their spirit, and their state,
Their being was a donative from you.
ARRUNTIUS
Well worded, and most like an orator.
TIBERIUS
Is this true, Silius?
SILIUS   Save thy question, Cæsar.
Thy spy, of famous credit, hath affirmed it.   285
ARRUNTIUS
Excellent Roman!

257 *crispèd* with stiff curled hair
278 *mutined* mutinied
282 *donative* gift (Latin *donativum*, imperial largesse)

257 *Roman eagles.* The image of an eagle formed the legionary standard.
286 *Excellent Roman!* Cf. 347, where Arruntius' *Excellent wolf* is probably
    not simply intensive, but an ironic glance back at this line.

SABINUS   He doth answer stoutly.

SEJANUS

If this be so, there needs no farther cause
Of crime against him.

VARRO   What can more impeach
The royal dignity, and state of Cæsar,
Than to be urgèd with a benefit   290
He cannot pay?

COTTA   In this, all Cæsar's fortune
Is made unequal to the courtesy.

LATIARIS

His means are clean destroyed, that should requite.

GALLUS

Nothing is great enough for Silius' merit.

ARRUNTIUS

Gallus on that side too?

SILIUS   Come, do not hunt,   295
And labour so about for circumstance,
To make him guilty, whom you have foredoomed:
Take shorter ways, I'll meet your purposes.
The words were mine, and more I now will say:
Since I have done thee that great service, Cæsar,   300
Thou still hast feared me; and, in place of grace,
Returned me hatred: so soon, all best turns,
With doubtful princes, turn deep injuries
In estimation, when they greater rise,
Than can be answered. Benefits, with you,   305
Are of no longer pleasure, than you can
With ease restore them; that transcended once,
Your studies are not how to thank, but kill.
It is your nature, to have all men slaves
To you, but you acknowledging to none.   310
The means that makes your greatness, must not come
In mention of it; if it do, it takes
So much away, you think: and that, which helped,
Shall soonest perish, if it stand in eye,
Where it may front, or but upbraid the high.   315

COTTA

Suffer him speak no more.

VARRO   Note but his spirit.

AFER

This shows him in the rest.

LATIARIS   Let him be censured.

288 *crime* accusation (Latin *crimen*)   297 *foredoomed* prejudged
302 *turns* services (cf. 'a good turn')   315 *front* affront

SEJANUS

   He hath spoke enough to prove him Cæsar's foe.

COTTA

   His thoughts look through his words.

SEJANUS   A censure.

SILIUS   Stay,

   Stay, most officious Senate, I shall straight   320

   Delude thy fury. Silius hath not placed

   His guards within him, against Fortune's spite,

   So weakly, but he can escape your grip

   That are but hands of Fortune: she herself

   When virtue doth oppose, must lose her threats.   325

   All that can happen in humanity,

   The frown of Cæsar, proud Sejanus' hatred,

   Base Varro's spleen, and Afer's bloodying tongue,

   The Senate's servile flattery, and these

   Mustered to kill, I am fortified against;   330

   And can look down upon: they are beneath me.

   It is not life whereof I stand enamoured:

   Nor shall my end make me accuse my fate.

   The coward, and the valiant man must fall,

   Only the cause, and manner how, discerns them: 335

   Which then are gladdest, when they cost us dearest.

   Romans, if any here be in this Senate,

   Would know to mock Tiberius' tyranny,

   Look upon Silius, and so learn to die.

                       [Stabs himself]

VARRO

   O, desperate act!

ARRUNTIUS   An honourable hand!   340

TIBERIUS

   Look, is he dead?

SABINUS   'Twas nobly struck, and home.

ARRUNTIUS

   My thought did prompt him to it. Farewell, Silius.

   Be famous ever for thy great example.

TIBERIUS

   We are not pleased, in this sad accident,

   That thus hath stalled, and abused our mercy,   345

   Intended to preserve thee, noble Roman:

   And to prevent thy hopes.

---

342 *My thought . . . to it.* Arruntius later committed suicide when accused
   by Macro. Cf. also V, 750f.

ARRUNTIUS   Excellent wolf!
  Now he is full, he howls.
SEJANUS   Cæsar doth wrong
  His dignity, and safety, thus to mourn
  The deserved end of so professed a traitor,   350
  And doth, by this his lenity, instruct
  Others as factious, to the like offence.
TIBERIUS
  The confiscation merely of his state
  Had been enough.
ARRUNTIUS   O, that was gaped for then?
VARRO
  Remove the body.
SEJANUS   Let citation   355
  Go out for Sosia.
GALLUS   Let her be proscribed.
  And for the goods, I think it fit that half
  Go to the treasure, half unto the children.
LEPIDUS
  With leave of Cæsar, I would think, that fourth
  Part, which the law doth cast on the informers,   360
  Should be enough; the rest go to the children:
  Wherein the Prince shall show humanity,
  And bounty, not to force them by their want
  (Which in their parent's trespass they deserved)
  To take ill courses.
TIBERIUS   It shall please us.
ARRUNTIUS   Ay,   365
  Out of necessity. This Lepidus
  Is grave and honest, and I have observed
  A moderation still in all his censures.
SABINUS
  And bending to the better—stay, who's this?
  Cremutius Cordus? what? is he brought in?   370
ARRUNTIUS
  More blood unto the banquet? Noble Cordus,
  I wish thee good: be as thy writings, free,
  And honest.
TIBERIUS   What is he?
SEJANUS   For th'annals, Cæsar.

    [*Enter*] PRÆCO, CORDUS, SATRIUS, NATTA
PRÆCO
  Cremutius Cordus.

351 *lenity* lenience   358 *treasure* public treasury

CORDUS   Here.

PRÆCO   Satrius Secundus,
Pinnarius Natta, you are his accusers.   375

ARRUNTIUS
Two of Sejanus' blood-hounds, whom he breeds
With human flesh, to bay at citizens.

AFER
Stand forth before the Senate, and confront him.

SATRIUS
I do accuse thee here, Cremutius Cordus,
To be a man factious, and dangerous,   380
A sower of sedition in the State,
A turbulent, and discontented spirit,
Which I will prove from thine own writings, here,
The annals thou hast published; where thou bite'st
The present age, and with a viper's tooth,   385
Being a member of it, dare'st that ill
Which never yet degenerous bastard did
Upon his parent.

NATTA   To this, I subscribe;
And, forth a world of more particulars,
Instance in only one: comparing men,   390
And times, thou praisest Brutus, and affirm'st
That Cassius was the last of all the Romans.

COTTA
How! what are we then?

VARRO   What is Cæsar? nothing?

AFER
My lords, this strikes at every Roman's private,
In whom reigns gentry, and estate of spirit,   395
To have a Brutus brought in parallel,
A parricide, an enemy of his country,
Ranked, and preferred to any real worth
That Rome now holds. This is most strangely invective.
Most full of spite, and insolent upbraiding.   400
Nor is't the time alone is here disprised,
But the whole man of time, yea Cæsar's self
Brought in disvalue; and he aimed at most
By oblique glance of his licentious pen.
Cæsar, if Cassius were the last of Romans,   405
Thou hast no name.

385 *with a viper's tooth* ungratefully
387 *degenerous* unworthily of family (Latin *degener*)
389 *forth* out of   394 *private* personal concern
397 *parricide* traitor (Latin *parricida*)   401 *disprised* held in contempt

TIBERIUS   Let's hear him answer. Silence.
CORDUS
So innocent I am of fact, my lords,
As but my words are argued; yet those words
Not reaching either prince, or prince's parent:
The which your law of treason comprehends.   410
Brutus, and Cassius, I am charged, t' have praised:
Whose deeds, when many more, besides myself,
Have writ, not one hath mentioned without honour.
Great Titus Livius, great for eloquence,
And faith, amongst us, in his history,   415
With so great praises Pompey did extol,
As oft Augustus called him a Pompeian:
Yet this not hurt their friendship. In his book
He often names Scipio, Afranius,
Yea, the same Cassius, and this Brutus too,   420
As worthi'st men; not thieves, and parricides,
Which notes, upon their fames, are now imposed.
Asinius Pollio's writings quite throughout
Give them a noble memory; so Messalla
Renowned his general Cassius: yet both these   425
Lived with Augustus, full of wealth, and honours.
To Cicero's book, where Cato was heaved up
Equal with heav'n, what else did Cæsar answer,
Being then Dictator, but with a penned oration,
As if before the judges? Do but see   430
Antonius' letters; read but Brutus' pleadings:
What vile reproach they hold against Augustus,
False I confess, but with much bitterness.
The epigrams of Bibaculus, and Catullus,
Are read, full stuffed with spite of both the Cæsars;   435
Yet deified Julius, and no less Augustus!
Both bore them, and contemned them: (I not know
Promptly to speak it, whether done with more
Temper, or wisdom) for such obloquies
If they despisèd be, they die suppressed,   440
But, if with rage acknowledged, they are confessed.
The Greeks I slip, whose licence not alone,
But also lust did 'scape unpunishèd:
Or where someone (by chance) exception took,
He words with words revenged. But, in my work,   445
What could be aimed more free, or farther off
From the time's scandal, than to write of those,

410 *comprehends* includes
422 *notes* titles

Whom death from grace, or hatred had exempted?
Did I, with Brutus, and with Cassius,
Armed, and possessed of the Philippi fields,   450
Incense the people in the civil cause,
With dangerous speeches? or do they, being slain
Seventy years since, as by their images
(Which not the conqueror hath defaced) appears,
Retain that guilty memory with writers?   455
Posterity pays every man his honour.
Nor shall there want, though I condemnèd am,
That will not only Cassius well approve,
And of great Brutus' honour mindful be,
But that will, also, mention make of me.   460

ARRUNTIUS
Freely, and nobly spoken.

SABINUS   With good temper,
I like him, that he is not moved with passion.

ARRUNTIUS
He puts 'em to their whisper.

TIBERIUS   Take him hence,
We shall determine of him at next sitting.

COTTA
Meantime, give order, that his books be burnt,   465
To the Ædiles.

SEJANUS   You have well advised.

AFER
It fits not such licentious things should live
T'upbraid the age.

ARRUNTIUS   If th'age were good, they might.

LATIARIS
Let 'em be burnt.

GALLUS   All sought, and burnt, today.

PRÆCO
The court is up, Lictors, resume the fasces.   470
          [*Exeunt, leaving*] ARRUNTIUS, SABINUS, LEPIDUS

ARRUNTIUS
Let 'em be burnt! O, how ridiculous
Appears the Senate's brainless diligence,
Who think they can, with present power, extinguish
The memory of all succeeding times!

SABINUS
'Tis true, when (contrary) the punishment   475
Of wit, doth make th'authority increase.
Nor do they aught, that use this cruelty

Of interdiction, and this rage of burning;
But purchase to themselves rebuke, and shame,
And to the writers an eternal name.   480
LEPIDUS
It is an argument the times are sore,
When virtue cannot safely be advanced;
Nor vice reproved.
ARRUNTIUS   Ay, noble Lepidus,
Augustus well foresaw, what we should suffer,
Under Tiberius, when he did pronounce   485
The Roman race most wretched, that should live
Between so slow jaws, and so long a-bruising.   [*Exeunt*]

[Act III, Scene ii]

[A room in the Palace. Enter] TIBERIUS, SEJANUS

TIBERIUS
This business hath succeeded well, Sejanus:
And quite removed all jealousy of practice
'Gainst Agrippina, and our nephews. Now,   490
We must bethink us how to plant our engines
For th'other pair, Sabinus, and Arruntius,
And Gallus too (how e'er he flatter us,)
His heart we know.
SEJANUS   Give it some respite, Cæsar.
Time shall mature, and bring to perfect crown,   495
What we, with so good vultures, have begun:
Sabinus shall be next.
TIBERIUS   Rather Arruntius.
SEJANUS
By any means, preserve him. His frank tongue
Being lent the reins, will take away all thought
Of malice, in your course against the rest.   500
We must keep him to stalk with.
TIBERIUS   Dearest head,
To thy most fortunate design I yield it.
SEJANUS
Sir—I have been so long trained up in grace,
First, with your father, great Augustus, since,

485 *pronounce* Q (F pronouuce)
502 *fortunate* Q (F forunate)

---

496 *vultures.* Birds of augury, with a further reference to the role played by
Afer and Varro. Cf. IV, 140.

With your most happy bounties so familiar,   505
As I not sooner would commit my hopes
Or wishes to the gods, than to your ears.
Nor have I ever, yet, been covetous
Of overbright, and dazzling honours: rather
To watch, and travail in great Cæsar's safety,   510
With the most common soldier.
TIBERIUS   'Tis confessed.
SEJANUS
The only gain, and which I count most fair
Of all my fortunes, is that mighty Cæsar
Hath thought me worthy his alliance. Hence
Begin my hopes.
TIBERIUS   H'mh?
SEJANUS   I have heard, Augustus   515
In the bestowing of his daughter, thought
But even of gentlemen of Rome: if so,
(I know not how to hope so great a favour)
But if a husband should be sought for Livia,
And I be had in mind, as Cæsar's friend,   520
I would but use the glory of the kindred.
It should not make me slothful, or less caring
For Cæsar's state; it were enough to me
It did confirm, and strengthen my weak house,
Against the now unequal opposition   525
Of Agrippina; and for dear regard
Unto my children, this I wish: myself
Have no ambition farther, than to end
My days in service of so dear a master.
TIBERIUS
We cannot but commend thy piety,   530
Most loved Sejanus, in acknowledging
Those bounties; which we, faintly, such remember.
But to thy suit. The rest of mortal men,
In all their drifts, and counsels, pursue profit:
Princes, alone, are of a different sort,   535
Directing their main actions still to fame.
We therefore will take time to think, and answer.
For Livia, she can best, herself, resolve

517 *But even* equal (to a nobleman)   520 *friend* Q (F freind)
521 *kindred* kinship   530 *piety* filial duty (Latin *pietas*)

515 Jonson explains in a marginal note, *His daughter was betrothed to Claudius, his son.* Julia was married to Claudius Marcellus before she married Tiberius. The note, in Latin in Q, is quoted from Lipsius.

If she will marry, after Drusus, or
Continue in the family; besides   540
She hath a mother, and a granddame yet,
Whose nearer counsels she may guide her by:
But I will simply deal. That enmity,
Thou fear'st in Agrippina, would burn more,
If Livia's marriage should (as 'twere in parts)   545
Divide th'imperial house; an emulation
Between the women might break forth: and discord
Ruin the sons, and nephews, on both hands.
What if it cause some present difference?
Thou art not safe, Sejanus, if thou prove it.   550
Canst thou believe, that Livia, first the wife
To Caius Cæsar, then my Drusus, now
Would be contented to grow old with thee,
Born but a private gentleman of Rome?
And raise thee with her loss, if not her shame?   555
Or say, that I should wish it, canst thou think
The Senate, or the people (who have seen
Her brother, father, and our ancestors,
In highest place of empire) will endure it?
The state thou hold'st already, is in talk;   560
Men murmur at thy greatness; and the nobles
Stick not, in public, to upbraid thy climbing
Above our father's favours, or thy scale:
And dare accuse me, from their hate to thee.
Be wise, dear friend. We would not hide these things   565
For friendship's dear respect. Nor will we stand
Adverse to thine, or Livia's designments.
What we had purposed to thee, in our thought,
And with what near degrees of love to bind thee,
And make thee equal to us; for the present,   570
We will forbear to speak. Only, thus much
Believe, our loved Sejanus, we not know
That height in blood, or honour, which thy virtue,
And mind to us, may not aspire with merit.
And this we'll publish, on all watched occasion   575
The Senate, or the people shall present.
SEJANUS
I am restored, and to my sense again,
Which I had lost in this so blinding suit.
Cæsar hath taught me better to refuse,
Than I knew how to ask. How pleaseth Cæsar   580

546 *emulation* rivalry   550 *prove* attempt, try
563 *scale* relative size, magnitude   575 *watched* public

T'embrace my late advice, for leaving Rome?
TIBERIUS
We are resolved.
SEJANUS   Here are some motives more
Which I have thought on since, may more confirm.
TIBERIUS
Careful Sejanus! we will straight peruse them:
Go forward in our main design, and prosper.   [*Exit*]   585
SEJANUS
If those but take, I shall: dull, heavy Cæsar!
Wouldst thou tell me, thy favours were made crimes?
And that my fortunes were esteemed thy faults?
That thou, for me, wert hated? and not think
I would with wingèd haste prevent that change,   590
When thou might'st win all to thyself again,
By forfeiture of me? Did those fond words
Fly swifter from thy lips, than this my brain,
This sparkling forge, created me an armour
T'encounter chance, and thee? Well, read my charms,   595
And may they lay that hold upon thy senses,
As thou had'st snuffed up hemlock, or ta'en down
The juice of poppy, and of mandrakes. Sleep,
Voluptuous Cæsar, and security
Seize on thy stupid powers, and leave them dead   600
To public cares, awake but to thy lusts.
The strength of which makes thy libidinous soul
Itch to leave Rome; and I have thrust it on:
With blaming of the city business,
The multitude of suits, the confluence   605
Of suitors, then their importunacies,
The manifold distractions he must suffer,
Besides ill rumours, envies, and reproaches,
All which, a quiet and retirèd life,
(Larded with ease, and pleasure) did avoid;   610
And yet, for any weighty, and great affair,
The fittest place to give the soundest counsels.
By this, shall I remove him both from thought,
And knowledge of his own most dear affairs;
Draw all dispatches through my private hands;   615
Know his designments, and pursue mine own;
Make mine own strengths, by giving suits, and places;
Conferring dignities, and offices:

597f. *hemlock . . . mandrakes* opiates.
606 *importunacies* requests

And these, that hate me now, wanting access
To him, will make their envy none, or less.   620
For when they see me arbiter of all,
They must observe: or else, with Cæsar fall.   *[Exit]*

                    [Enter] TIBERIUS

TIBERIUS
To marry Livia? will no less, Sejanus,
Content thy aims? no lower object? well!
Thou know'st how thou art wrought into our trust;   625
Woven in our design; and think'st, we must
Now use thee, whatsoe'er thy projects are:
'Tis true. But yet with caution, and fit care.
And, now we better think—who's there, within?

                    [Enter SERVUS]

SERVUS
Cæsar?
TIBERIUS To leave our journey off, were sin   630
'Gainst our decreed delights; and would appear
Doubt: or (what less becomes a prince) low fear.
Yet, doubt hath law, and fears have their excuse,
Where princes' states plead necessary use;
As ours doth now: more in Sejanus' pride,   635
Than all fell Agrippina's hates beside.
Those are the dreadful enemies, we raise
With favours, and make dangerous, with praise;
The injured by us may have will alike,
But 'tis the favourite hath the power, to strike: 640
And fury ever boils more high, and strong,
Heat with ambition, than revenge of wrong.
'Tis then a part of supreme skill, to grace
No man too much; but hold a certain space
Between th'ascender's rise, and thine own flat,   645
Lest, when all rounds be reached, his aim be that.
'Tis thought—is Macro in the palace? See:
If not, go, seek him, to come to us—He   *[Exit* SERVUS]
Must be the organ, we must work by now;
Though none less apt for trust: need doth allow   650
What choice would not. I have heard, that aconite

642 *Heat* heated
646 *rounds* rungs of a ladder
651 *aconite* a poisonous plant.

Being timely taken, hath a healing might
Against the scorpion's stroke; the proof we'll give:
That, while two poisons wrestle, we may live.
He hath a spirit too working, to be used   655
But to th'encounter of his like; excused
Are wiser sovereigns then, that raise one ill
Against another, and both safely kill:
The prince, that feeds great natures, they will sway him;
Who nourisheth a lion, must obey him.   660

                [*Enter*] MACRO, [SERVUS]

Macro, we sent for you.
MACRO   I heard so, Cæsar.
TIBERIUS
   (Leave us awhile.) [*Exit* SERVUS] When you shall know,
                                   good Macro,
   The causes of our sending, and the ends;
   You then will harken nearer: and be pleased
   You stand so high, both in our choice, and trust.   665
MACRO
   The humblest place in Cæsar's choice, or trust,
   May make glad Macro proud; without ambition:
   Save to do Cæsar service.
TIBERIUS   Leave our courtings.
   We are in purpose, Macro, to depart
   The city for a time, and see Campania;   670
   Not for our pleasures, but to dedicate
   A pair of temples, one, to Jupiter
   At Capua, th'other at Nola, to Augustus:
   In which great work, perhaps, our stay will be
   Beyond our will produced. Now, since we are   675
   Not ignorant what danger may be born
   Out of our shortest absence, in a state
   So subject unto envy, and embroiled
   With hate, and faction; we have thought on thee,
   (Amongst a field of Romans,) worthiest Macro,   680
   To be our eye, and ear, to keep strict watch
   On Agrippina, Nero, Drusus, ay,
   And on Sejanus: not, that we distrust
   His loyalty, or do repent one grace,
   Of all that heap, we have conferred on him.   685
   (For that were to disparage our election,
   And call that judgement now in doubt, which then

668 *our* of us
675 *produced* extended

Seemed as unquestioned as an oracle,)
But, greatness hath his cankers. Worms, and moths
Breed out of too fit matter, in the things   690
Which after they consume, transferring quite
The substance of their makers, int' themselves.
Macro is sharp, and apprehends. Besides,
I know him subtle, close, wise, and well read
In man, and his large nature. He hath studied   695
Affections, passions, knows their springs, their ends,
Which way, and whether they will work: 'tis proof
Enough, of his great merit, that we trust him.
Then, to a point; (because our conference
Cannot be long without suspicion)   700
Here, Macro, we assign thee, both to spy,
Inform, and chastise; think, and use thy means,
Thy ministers, what, where, on whom thou wilt;
Explore, plot, practise: all thou dost in this,
Shall be, as if the Senate, or the laws   705
Had giv'n it privilege, and thou thence styled
The saviour both of Cæsar, and of Rome.
We will not take thy answer, but in act;
Whereto, as thou proceed'st, we hope to hear
By trusted messengers. If't be enquired,   710
Wherefore we called you, say, you have in charge
To see our chariots ready, and our horse:
Be still our loved, and (shortly) honoured Macro.   [*Exit*]
MACRO
I will not ask, why Cæsar bids do this:
But joy, that he bids me. It is the bliss   715
Of courts, to be employed; no matter, how:
A prince's power makes all his actions virtue.
We, whom he works by, are dumb instruments,
To do, but not enquire: his great intents
Are to be served, not searched. Yet, as that bow   720
Is most in hand, whose owner best doth know
T'affect his aims, so let that statesman hope
Most use, most price, can hit his prince's scope.
Nor must he look at what, or whom to strike,
But loose at all; each mark must be alike.   725
Were it to plot against the fame, the life
Of one, with whom I twinned; remove a wife

707 *saviour* Q (F savier, edd. saver)
722 *affect* obtain   723 *scope* target
725 *loose* Q (F lose) discharge arrow
    mark target

From my warm side, as loved, as is the air;
Practise away each parent; draw mine heir
In compass, though but one; work all my kin 730
To swift perdition; leave no untrained engine,
For friendship, or for innocence; nay, make
The gods all guilty: I would undertake
This, being imposed me, both with gain, and ease.
The way to rise, is to obey, and please. 735
He that will thrive in state, he must neglect
The trodden paths, that truth and right respect;
And prove new, wilder ways: for virtue, there,
Is not that narrow thing, she is elsewhere.
Men's fortune there is virtue; reason, their will: 740
Their licence, law; and their observance, skill.
Occasion, is their foil; conscience, their stain;
Profit, their lustre: and what else is, vain.
If then it be the lust of Cæsar's power,
T'have raised Sejanus up, and in an hour 745
O'erturn him, tumbling, down, from height of all;
We are his ready engine: and his fall
May be our rise. It is no uncouth thing
To see fresh buildings from old ruins spring.   [*Exit*]

CHORUS—OF MUSICIANS

[Act IV, Scene i]

[*Agrippina's house. Enter*] GALLUS, AGRIPPINA

GALLUS
   You must have patience, royal Agrippina.
AGRIPPINA
   I must have vengeance, first: and that were nectar
   Unto my famished spirits. O, my fortune,
   Let it be sudden thou prepare'st against me;
   Strike all my powers of understanding blind, 5
   And ignorant of destiny to come:
   Let me not fear, that cannot hope.
GALLUS   Dear Princess,
   These tyrannies, on yourself, are worse than Cæsar's.
AGRIPPINA
   Is this the happiness of being born great?

729f. *draw . . . in compass* trap
742 *Occasion, is their foil* opportunity is the track they follow
748 *uncouth* unknown

Still to be aimed at? still to be suspected?   10
To live the subject of all jealousies?
At the least colour made, if not the ground
To every painted danger? who would not
Choose once to fall, than thus to hang forever?
GALLUS
You might be safe, if you would—
AGRIPPINA   What, my Gallus?   15
Be lewd Sejanus' strumpet? Or the bawd
To Cæsar's lusts, he now is gone to practise?
Not these are safe, where nothing is. Yourself,
While thus you stand but by me, are not safe.
Was Silius safe? or the good Sosia safe?   20
Or was my niece, dear Claudia Pulchra safe?
Or innocent Furnius? They, that latest have
(By being made guilty) added reputation
To Afer's eloquence? O, foolish friends,
Could not so fresh example warn your loves,   25
But you must buy my favours, with that loss
Unto yourselves: and, when you might perceive
That Cæsar's cause of raging must forsake him,
Before his will? Away, good Gallus, leave me.
Here to be seen, is danger; to speak, treason: 30
To do me least observance, is called faction.
You are unhappy in me, and I in all.
Where are my sons? Nero? and Drusus? We
Are they, be shot at; let us fall apart:
Not, in our ruins, sepulchre our friends.   35
Or shall we do some action, like offence,
To mock their studies, that would make us faulty?
And frustrate practice, by preventing it?
The danger's like: for, what they can contrive,
They will make good. No innocence is safe,   40
When power contests. Nor can they trespass more,
Whose only being was all crime, before.

[*Enter* NERO, DRUSUS JUNIOR, CALIGULA]

37 *studies* schemes
39 *like* the same

12f. *colour made . . . painted danger?* Said to be the particular hue, if not the
    very background colour, of every painted danger (alleged plot).
34 *Are they, be shot at.* To be shot at, i.e., we share their peril, and they
    ours.
    fall apart. Meet our doom separately.

R—D

NERO
　　You hear, Sejanus is come back from Cæsar?
GALLUS
　　No. How? Disgraced?
DRUSUS JUNIOR　　　　　　　More gracèd now, than ever.
GALLUS
　　By what mischance?
CALIGULA　　　　　　　　A fortune, like enough　　　　　　　45
　　Once to be bad.
DRUSUS JUNIOR　　　But turned too good, to both.
GALLUS
　　What was't?
NERO　　　　　　Tiberius sitting at his meat,
　　In a farmhouse, they call Spelunca, sited
　　By the seaside, among the Fundane hills,
　　Within a natural cave, part of the grot　　　　　　　50
　　(About the entry) fell, and overwhelmed
　　Some of the waiters; others ran away:
　　Only Sejanus, with his knees, hands, face,
　　O'erhanging Cæsar, did oppose himself
　　To the remaining ruins, and was found　　　　　　　55
　　In that so labouring posture, by the soldiers
　　That came to succour him. With which adventure,
　　He hath so fixed himself in Cæsar's trust,
　　As thunder cannot move him, and is come
　　With all the height of Cæsar's praise, to Rome.　　　60
AGRIPPINA
　　And power, to turn those ruins all on us;
　　And bury whole posterities beneath them.
　　Nero, and Drusus, and Caligula,
　　Your places are the next, and therefore most
　　In their offence. Think on your birth, and blood,　　65
　　Awake your spirits, meet their violence,
　　'Tis princely, when a tyrant doth oppose;
　　And is a fortune sent to exercise
　　Your virtue, as the wind doth try strong trees:
　　Who by vexation grow more sound, and firm.　　　70
　　After your father's fall, and uncle's fate,
　　What can you hope, but all the change of stroke
　　That force, or slight can give? Then stand upright;
　　And though you do not act, yet suffer nobly:
　　Be worthy of my womb, and take strong cheer;　　75
　　What we do know will come, we should not fear. [*Exeunt*]

47 *meat* meal

[Act IV, Scene ii]

[*The Street. Enter*] MACRO

MACRO
    Returned so soon? renewed in trust, and grace?
    Is Cæsar then so weak? or hath the place
    But wrought this alteration, with the air;
    And he, on next remove, will all repair?   80
    Macro, thou art engaged: and what before
    Was public; now, must be thy private, more.
    The weal of Cæsar, fitness did imply;
    But thine own fate confers necessity
    On thy employment: and the thoughts born nearest   85
    Unto ourselves, move swiftest still, and dearest.
    If he recover, thou art lost: yea, all
    The weight of preparation to his fall
    Will turn on thee, and crush thee. Therefore, strike
    Before he settle, to prevent the like   90
    Upon thyself. He doth his vantage know,
    That makes it home, and gives the foremost blow.   [*Exit*]

[Act IV, Scene iii]

[*Agrippina's house. Enter*] LATIARIS, RUFUS, OPSIUS

LATIARIS
    It is a service, great Sejanus will
    See well requited, and accept of nobly.
    Here place yourselves, between the roof, and ceiling,   95
    And when I bring him to his words of danger,
    Reveal yourselves, and take him.
RUFUS   Is he come?
LATIARIS
    I'll now go fetch him.   [*Exit*]

---

92 *foremost* first

---

80 *on next . . . all repair?* At the next stage of his journey will make every-
    thing as it was before.
95 According to Tacitus, 'they put their ears to the cracks'; probably the
    actors playing the spies remained on the upper stage of the Jacobean
    playhouse from their entrance until IV, 217, following Tacitus' des-
    cription at IV, 114.

OPSIUS   With good speed. I long
  To merit from the State, in such an action.
RUFUS
  I hope, it will obtain the Consulship   100
  For one of us.
OPSIUS   We cannot think of less,
  To bring in one, so dangerous as Sabinus.
RUFUS
  He was a follower of Germanicus,
  And still is an observer of his wife,
  And children, though they be declined in grace;   105
  A daily visitant, keeps them company
  In private, and in public; and is noted
  To be the only client, of the house:
  Pray Jove, he will be free to Latiaris.
OPSIUS
  He's allied to him, and doth trust him well.   110
RUFUS
  And he'll requite his trust?
OPSIUS   To do an office
  So grateful to the State, I know no man
  But would strain nearer bands, than kindred—
RUFUS   List,
  I hear them come.
OPSIUS   Shift to our holes, with silence. [*Exeunt*]

          [*Enter*] LATIARIS, SABINUS

LATIARIS
  It is a noble constancy you show   115
  To this afflicted house: that not like others,
  (The friends of season) you do follow fortune,
  And in the winter of their fate, forsake
  The place, whose glories warmed you. You are just,
  And worthy such a princely patron's love,   120
  As was the world's renowned Germanicus:
  Whose ample merit when I call to thought,
  And see his wife, and issue, objects made
  To so much envy, jealousy, and hate;
  It makes me ready to accuse the gods   125
  Of negligence, as men of tyranny.
SABINUS
  They must be patient, so must we.

104 *observer* partisan
110 *allied* related
117 *friends of season* 'fair weather friends'

LATIARIS   O Jove.
   What will become of us, or of the times,
   When, to be high, or noble, are made crimes?
   When land, and treasure are most dangerous faults?   130
SABINUS
   Nay, when our table, yea our bed assaults
   Our peace, and safety? when our writings are,
   By any envious instruments (that dare
   Apply them to the guilty) made to speak
   What they will have, to fit their tyrannous wreak?   135
   When ignorance is scarcely innocence:
   And knowledge made a capital offence?
   When not so much, but the bare empty shade
   Of liberty, is reft us? and we made,
   The prey to greedy vultures, and vile spies,   140
   That first, transfix us with their murdering eyes?
LATIARIS
   Me thinks, the genius of the Roman race
   Should not be so extinct, but that bright flame
   Of liberty might be revived again,
   (Which no good man but with his life, should lose)   145
   And we not sit like spent, and patient fools,
   Still puffing in the dark, at one poor coal,
   Held on by hope, till the last spark is out.
   The cause is public, and the honour, name,
   The immortality of every soul   150
   That is not bastard, or a slave in Rome,
   Therein concerned: whereto, if men would change
   The wearied arm, and for the weighty shield
   So long sustained, employ the ready sword,
   We might have some assurance of our vows.   155
   This ass's fortitude doth tire us all.
   It must be active valour must redeem
   Our loss, or none. The rock, and our hard steel
   Should meet, t'enforce those glorious fires again,
   Whose splendour cheered the world, and heat gave life   160
   No less than doth the sun's.
SABINUS   'Twere better stay,
   In lasting darkness, and despair of day.
   No ill should force the subject undertake
   Against the sovereign, more than hell should make
   The gods do wrong. A good man should, and must   165
   Sit rather down with loss, than rise unjust.

139 *reft* or 'left'?

Though, when the Romans first did yield themselves
To one man's power, they did not mean their lives,
Their fortunes, and their liberties, should be
His absolute spoil, as purchased by the sword.   170

LATIARIS
Why we are worse, if to be slaves, and bond
To Cæsar's slave, be such, the proud Sejanus!
He that is all, does all, gives Cæsar leave
To hide his ulcerous, and anointed face,
With his bald crown at Rhodes, while he here stalks   175
Upon the heads of Romans, and their princes,
Familiarly to empire.

SABINUS   Now you touch
A point indeed, wherein he shows his art,
As well as power.

LATIARIS   And villany in both.
Do you observe where Livia lodges? How   180
Drusus came dead? What men have been cut off?

SABINUS
Yes, those are things removed: I nearer looked,
Into his later practice, where he stands
Declared a master in his mystery.
First, ere Tiberius went, he wrought his fear   185
To think that Agrippina sought his death.
Then put those doubts in her; sent her oft word,
Under the show of friendship, to beware
Of Cæsar, for he laid to poison her:
Drove them to frowns, to mutual jealousies,   190
Which, now, in visible hatred are burst out.
Since, he hath had his hirèd instruments
To work on Nero, and to heave him up;
To tell him Cæsar's old; that all the people,
Yea, all the army have their eyes on him;   195
That both do long to have him undertake
Something of worth, to give the world a hope;
Bids him to court their grace: the easy youth,
Perhaps, gives ear, which straight he writes to Cæsar;
And with this comment; 'See yond dangerous boy;   200
Note but the practice of the mother, there;
She's tying him, for purposes at hand,

177 *Familiarly to empire* to rule unceremoniously   189 *laid* planned

---

175 *Rhodes*. A rare error of history in the play; Tiberius' exile in Rhodes
  took place during the reign of Augustus.
202f. *tying him . . . of sword*. She is allying him with fighters, for a coming time of need.

With men of sword.' Here's Cæsar put in fright
'Gainst son, and mother. Yet, he leaves not thus.
The second brother Drusus (a fierce nature,   205
And fitter for his snares, because ambitious,
And full of envy) him he clasps, and hugs,
Poisons with praise, tells him what hearts he wears,
How bright he stands in popular expectance;
That Rome doth suffer with him, in the wrong   210
His mother does him, by preferring Nero:
Thus sets he them asunder, each 'gainst other,
Projects the course, that serves him to condemn,
Keeps in opinion of a friend to all,
And all drives on to ruin.

LATIARIS   Cæsar sleeps,   215
And nods at this?

SABINUS   Would he might ever sleep,
Bogged in his filthy lusts.

                  [*Enter* OPSIUS *and* RUFUS]

OPSIUS   Treason to Cæsar.

RUFUS
Lay hands upon the traitor, Latiaris,
Or take the name thyself.

LATIARIS   I am for Cæsar.

SABINUS
Am I then catched?

RUFUS   How think you, sir? you are.   220

SABINUS
Spies of this head! so white! so full of years!
Well, my most reverend monsters, you may live
To see yourselves thus snared.

OPSIUS   Away with him.

LATIARIS
Hale him away.

RUFUS   To be a spy for traitors,
Is honourable vigilance.

SABINUS   You do well,   225
My most officious instruments of state;
Men of all uses: drag me hence, away.
The year is well begun, and I fall fit,
To be an offering to Sejanus. Go.

---

208 *what hearts he wears* what men are loyal to him

228f. Sabinus regards himself as a New Year's sacrifice to Sejanus, the new
     deity of Rome. The irony is heightened because by custom no execu-
     tions took place in the sacred first days of the year.

OPSIUS
    Cover him with his garments, hide his face.   230
SABINUS
    It shall not need. Forbear your rude assault,
    The fault's not shameful villany makes a fault.   [*Exeunt*]

[Act IV, Scene iv]

[*The Street. Enter*] MACRO, CALIGULA

MACRO
    Sir, but observe how thick your dangers meet
    In his clear drifts! Your mother, and your brothers,
    Now cited to the Senate! Their friend, Gallus,   235
    Feasted today by Cæsar, since committed!
    Sabinus, here we met, hurried to fetters!
    The Senators all struck with fear, and silence,
    Save those, whose hopes depend not on good means,
    But force their private prey, from public spoil!   240
    And you must know, if here you stay, your state
    Is sure to be the subject of his hate,
    As now the object.
CALIGULA   What would you advise me?
MACRO
    To go for Capreæ presently: and there
    Give up yourself, entirely, to your uncle.   245
    Tell Cæsar (since your mother is accused
    To fly for succours to Augustus' statue,
    And to the army, with your brethren) you
    Have rather chose, to place your aids in him,
    Than live suspected; or in hourly fear   250
    To be thrust out, by bold Sejanus' plots:
    Which, you shall confidently urge, to be
    Most full of peril to the state, and Cæsar,
    As being laid to his peculiar ends,
    And not to be let run, with common safety.   255
    All which (upon the second) I'll make plain,
    So both shall love, and trust with Cæsar gain.
CALIGULA
    Away then, let's prepare us for our journey.   [*Exeunt*]

[*Enter*] ARRUNTIUS

234 *drifts* plots
245 *uncle* Tiberius (really great-uncle, brother of Germanicus' father,
    Nero Drusus)
256 *upon the second* as a supporter

ARRUNTIUS
  Still, dost thou suffer heav'n? will no flame,
  Not heat of sin make thy just wrath to boil   260
  In thy distempered bosom, and o'erflow
  The pitchy blazes of impiety,
  Kindled beneath thy throne? Still canst thou sleep,
  Patient, while vice doth make an antic face
  At thy dread power, and blow dust, and smoke   265
  Into thy nostrils? Jove, will nothing wake thee?
  Must vile Sejanus pull thee by the beard,
  Ere thou wilt open thy black-lidded eye,
  And look him dead? Well! Snore on, dreaming gods:
  And let this last of that proud giant-race,   270
  Heave mountain upon mountain, 'gainst your state—
  Be good unto me, Fortune, and you powers,
  Whom I, expostulating, have profaned;
  I see (what's equal with a prodigy)
  A great, a noble Roman, and an honest,   275

[Enter LEPIDUS]

  Live an old man! O, Marcus Lepidus,
  When is our turn to bleed? Thyself, and I
  (Without our boast) are almost all the few
  Left, to be honest, in these impious times.
LEPIDUS
  What we are left to be, we will be, Lucius,   280
  Though tyranny did stare, as wide as death,
  To fright us from it.
ARRUNTIUS   'T hath so, on Sabinus.
LEPIDUS
  I saw him now drawn from the Gemonies,
  And (what increased the direness of the fact)
  His faithful dog (upbraiding all us Romans)   285
  Never forsook the corpse, but, seeing it thrown
  Into the stream, leaped in, and drowned with it.
ARRUNTIUS
  O act! to be envied him, of us men!
  We are the next, the hook lays hold on, Marcus:
  What are thy arts (good patriot, teach them me)   290
  That have preserved thy hairs, to this white dye,

---

264 *antic* ed. (F antique, a common 17th-century spelling)

---

270 *giant-race*. The sons of earth who tried to scale and conquer heaven by
    piling mountain upon mountain.

And kept so reverend, and so dear a head,
Safe, on his comely shoulders?
LEPIDUS   Arts, Arruntius?
None, but the plain, and passive fortitude,
To suffer, and be silent; never stretch   295
These arms, against the torrent; live at home,
With my own thoughts, and innocence about me,
Not tempting the wolves' jaws: these are my arts.
ARRUNTIUS
I would begin to study 'em, if I thought
They would secure me. May I pray to Jove,   300
In secret, and be safe? Ay, or aloud?
With open wishes? so I do not mention
Tiberius, or Sejanus? Yes, I must,
If I speak out. 'Tis hard, that. May I think,
And not be racked? What danger is't to dream?   305
Talk in one's sleep? or cough? who knows the law?
May I shake my head, without a comment? say
It rains, or it holds up, and not be thrown
Upon the Gemonies? These now are things,
Whereon men's fortune, yea their fate depends.   310
Nothing hath privilege 'gainst the violent ear.
No place, no day, no hour (we see) is free
(Not our religious, and most sacred times)
From some one kind of cruelty: all matter,
Nay all occasion pleaseth. Madmen's rage,   315
The idleness of drunkards, women's nothing,
Jesters' simplicity, all, all is good
That can be catched at. Nor is now th'event
Of any person, or for any crime,
To be expected; for, 'tis always one: 320
Death, with some little difference of place,
Or time—what's this? Prince Nero? guarded?

[*Enter*] LACO, NERO, [LICTORS]

LACO
On, Lictors, keep your way: my lords, forbear.
On pain of Cæsar's wrath, no man attempt
Speech with the prisoner.
NERO   Noble friends, be safe: 325
To lose yourselves for words, were as vain hazard,
As unto me small comfort: fare you well.
Would all Rome's sufferings in my fate did dwell.

318 *event* consequence, outcome (Latin *eventus*)
320 *expected* in doubt   326 *lose* ed. (Q, F loose)

LACO
    Lictors, away.
LEPIDUS   Where goes he, Laco?
LACO   Sir,
    He's banished into Pontia, by the Senate.   330
ARRUNTIUS
    Do I see? and hear? and feel? May I trust sense?
    Or doth my fant'sy form it?
LEPIDUS   Where's his brother?
LACO
    Drusus is prisoner in the palace.
ARRUNTIUS   Ha?
    I smell it now: 'tis rank. Where's Agrippina?
LACO
    The Princess is confined, to Pandataria.   335
ARRUNTIUS
    Bolts, Vulcan; bolts, for Jove! Phœbus, thy bow;
    Stern Mars, thy sword; and blue-eyed maid, thy spear;
    Thy club, Alcides: all the armoury
    Of heaven is too little!—Ha? to guard
    The gods, I meant. Fine, rare dispatch! This same   340
    Was swiftly born! confined? imprisoned? banished?
    Most tripartite! The cause, sir?
LACO   Treason.
ARRUNTIUS   O?
    The complement of all accusings? that
    Will hit, when all else fails.
LEPIDUS   This turn is strange!
    But yesterday, the people would not hear   345
    Far less objected, but cried, Cæsar's letters
    Were false, and forged; that all these plots were malice:
    And that the ruin of the Prince's house
    Was practised 'gainst his knowledge. Where are now
    Their voices? now, that they behold his heirs   350
    Locked up, disgraced, led into exile?
ARRUNTIUS   Hushed.
    Drowned in their bellies. Wild Sejanus' breath
    Hath, like a whirlwind, scattered that poor dust,
    With this rude blast.
                He turns to Laco, and the rest
                         We'll talk no treason, sir,
    If that be it you stand for? Fare you well.   355

---

337 *blue-eyed maid.* Pallas Athene, a warrior goddess; perhaps a misunderstanding of Homer's 'bright-eyed Athene'.

We have no need of horse-leeches. Good spy,
Now you are spied, be gone.
                              [*Exeunt* LACO, NERO, LICTORS]
LEPIDUS   I fear, you wrong him.
    He has the voice to be an honest Roman.
ARRUNTIUS
    And trusted to this office? Lepidus,
    I'd sooner trust Greek Sinon, than a man   360
    Our State employs. He's gone: and being gone,
    I dare tell you (whom I dare better trust)
    That our night-eyed Tiberius doth not see
    His minion's drifts; or, if he do, he's not
    So arrant subtle, as we fools do take him: 365
    To breed a mongrel up, in his own house,
    With his own blood, and (if the good gods please)
    At his own throat, flesh him, to take a leap.
    I do not beg it, heav'n: but, if the fates
    Grant it these eyes, they must not wink.
LEPIDUS   They must   370
    Not see it, Lucius.
ARRUNTIUS   Who should let 'em?
LEPIDUS   Zeal,
    And duty; with the thought, he is our prince.
ARRUNTIUS
    He is our monster: forfeited to vice
    So far, as no racked virtue can redeem him.
    His loathèd person fouler than all crimes: 375
    An emperor, only in his lusts. Retired
    (From all regard of his own fame, or Rome's)
    Into an obscure island; where he lives
    (Acting his tragedies with a comic face)
    Amidst his rout of Chaldees: spending hours,   380
    Days, weeks, and months, in the unkind abuse
    Of grave astrology, to the bane of men,
    Casting the scope of men's nativities,
    And having found ought worthy in their fortune,
    Kill, or precipitate them in the sea,   385

356 *horse-leeches.* Especially large medicinal leeches, hence insatiably
    greedy people.
368 *flesh him, to take a leap.* Reward him with a bit of flesh, to encourage him;
    part of the extensive imagery of hunting in this act, which is antici-
    pated in II, 406.
379 Tiberius acts out the tragedy of Rome and her people wearing a face
    like the lewd masks of late Roman comedies, one of which satirized
    Tiberius' retirement to Capreæ.

And boast, he can mock fate. Nay, muse not: these
Are far from ends of evil, scarce degrees.
He hath his slaughter-house, at Capreæ;
Where he doth study murder, as an art:
And they are dearest in his grace, that can   390
Devise the deepest tortures. Thither, too,
He hath his boys, and beauteous girls ta'en up,
Out of our noblest houses, the best formed,
Best nurtured, and most modest: what's their good
Serves to provoke his bad. Some are allured,   395
Some threatened; others (by their friends detained)
Are ravished hence, like captives, and, in sight
Of their most grievèd parents, dealt away
Unto his spintries, sellaries, and slaves,
Masters of strange, and new-commented lusts,   400
For which wise nature hath not left a name.
To this (what most strikes us, and bleeding Rome,)
He is, with all his craft, become the ward
To his own vassal, a stale catamite:
Whom he (upon our low, and suffering necks)   405
Hath raised, from excrement, to side the gods,
And have his proper sacrifice in Rome:
Which Jove beholds, and yet will sooner rive
A senseless oak with thunder, than his trunk.

                [*Enter*] LACO, POMPONIUS, MINUTIUS

                        To them

LACO
These letters make men doubtful what t'expect,   410
Whether his coming, or his death.
POMPONIUS   Troth, both:
And which comes soonest, thank the gods for.
(ARRUNTIUS   List,
Their talk is Cæsar, I would hear all voices.)
MINUTIUS
One day, he's well; and will return to Rome:
The next day, sick; and knows not when to hope it.   415

387 *degrees* steps toward it
400 *commented* invented (Latin *commentus*)
404 *catamite* sodomite
406 *to side* to stand alongside
407 *proper* own

---

399 *spintries, sellaries*. Male prostitutes and practitioners of unnatural vice;
     the words appear in Greenway's translation of Tacitus' *Annals*.

LACO
    True, and today, one of Sejanus' friends
    Honoured by special writ; and on the morrow
    Another punished—
POMPONIUS   By more special writ.
MINUTIUS
    This man receives his praises of Sejanus,
    A second, but slight mention: a third, none: 420
    A fourth, rebukes. And thus he leaves the Senate
    Divided, and suspended, all uncertain.
LACO
    These forkèd tricks, I understand 'em not,
    Would he would tell us whom he loves, or hates,
    That we might follow, without fear, or doubt.   425
(ARRUNTIUS
    Good Heliotrope! Is this your honest man?
    Let him be yours so still. He is my knave.)
POMPONIUS
    I cannot tell, Sejanus still goes on,
    And mounts, we see: new statues are advanced,
    Fresh leaves of titles, large inscriptions read,   430
    His fortune sworn by, himself new gone out
    Cæsar's colleague, in the fifth Consulship,
    More altars smoke to him, than all the gods:
    What would we more?
(ARRUNTIUS   That the dear smoke would choke him,
    That would I more.
LEPIDUS   Peace, good Arruntius.)   435
LACO
    But there are letters come (they say) ev'n now,
    Which do forbid that last.
MINUTIUS   Do you hear so?
LACO   Yes.
POMPONIUS
    By Pollux, that's the worst.
(ARRUNTIUS   By Hercules, best.)
MINUTIUS
    I did not like the sign, when Regulus,
    (Whom all we know no friend unto Sejanus)   440
    Did, by Tiberius' so precise command,

426 *Heliotrope.* A flower that follows the sun, therefore a symbol of oppor-
    tunism; but unusual in this sense. The more common association of the
    flower is, on the contrary, with the loyal follower, especially Christian,
    who shuts himself up in his master's absence.

Succeed a fellow in the Consulship:
It boded somewhat.
POMPONIUS   Not a mote. His partner,
Fulcinius Trio, is his own, and sure.
Here comes Terentius. He can give us more.   445

[Enter TERENTIUS]
They whisper with Terentius

LEPIDUS
I'll ne'er believe, but Cæsar hath some scent
Of bold Sejanus' footing. These cross points
Of varying letters, and opposing Consuls,
Mingling his honours, and his punishments,
Feigning now ill, now well, raising Sejanus,   450
And then depressing him, (as now of late
In all reports we have it) cannot be
Empty of practice: 'tis Tiberius' art.
For (having found his favourite grown too great,
And, with his greatness, strong; that all the soldiers 455
Are, with their leaders, made at his devotion;
That almost all the Senate are his creatures,
Or hold on him their main dependances,
Either for benefit, or hope, or fear;
And that himself hath lost much of his own,   460
By parting unto him; and by th'increase
Of his rank lusts, and rages, quite disarmed
Himself of love, or other public means,
To dare an open contestation)
His subtlety hath chose this doubling line,   465
To hold him even in: not so to fear him,

444 *his own* Sejanus'   447 *footing* established place
456 *made at his devotion* made devoted to him
461 *parting unto* sharing with
466 *even in* in check   *fear* frighten

---

438 In Q and the first state of F, this line read
    POMPONIUS
        By Castor, that's the worst.
    (ARRUNTIUS   By Pollux, best.)
In the same state, line 435 did not exist, and the parenthesis closed after
him. The addition of 435 in the corrected state merely clarifies the point
of Arruntius' remark, but the change in 438—the most substantial of all
the proof-corrections in F—is a classical nicety, for only women swore
by Castor, men by Hercules (Jonson made the same mistake in *Poetaster*
IV.i, 15, where in Q Cytheris swears by Hercules, but he corrected this
to Juno in the first state of F; in both places the hero's name must be
pronounced 'Herc'les'). The improvement in accuracy barely justifies
the loss of balance and wit.

As wholly put him out, and yet give check
Unto his farther boldness. In mean time,
By his employments, makes him odious
Unto the staggering rout, whose aid (in fine)   470
He hopes to use, as sure, who (when they sway)
Bear down, o'erturn all objects in their way.
ARRUNTIUS
You may be a Linceus, Lepidus: yet, I
See no such cause, but that a politic tyrant
(Who can so well disguise it) should have ta'en   475
A nearer way: fained honest, and come home
To cut his throat, by law.
LEPIDUS   Ay, but his fear
Would ne'er be masked, albe his vices were.
POMPONIUS
His lordship then is still in grace?
TERENTIUS   Assure you,
Never in more, either of grace, or power.   480
POMPONIUS
The gods are wise, and just.
(ARRUNTIUS   The fiends they are.
To suffer thee belie 'em?)
TERENTIUS   I have here
His last, and present letters, where he writes him
The 'partner of his cares', and 'his Sejanus'—
LACO
But is that true, it is prohibited,   485
To sacrifice unto him?
TERENTIUS   Some such thing
Cæsar makes scruple of, but forbids it not;
No more than to himself: says, he could wish
It were forborn to all.
LACO   Is it no other?
TERENTIUS
No other, on my trust. For your more surety,   490
Here is that letter too.
(ARRUNTIUS   How easily,
Do wretched men believe, what they would have!
Looks this like plot?
LEPIDUS   Noble Arruntius, stay.)
LACO
He names him here without his titles.
(LEPIDUS   Note.

478 *albe* although
485 *it is* edd. (Q, F it 'tis)

ARRUNTIUS
  Yes, and come off your notable fool. I will.)   495
LACO
  No other, than Sejanus.
POMPONIUS   That's but haste
  In him that writes. Here he gives large amends.
MINUTIUS
  And with his own hand written?
POMPONIUS   Yes.
LACO   Indeed?
TERENTIUS
  Believe it, gentlemen, Sejanus' breast
  Never received more full contentments in,   500
  Than at this present.
POMPONIUS   Takes he well th'escape
  Of young Caligula, with Macro?
TERENTIUS   Faith,
  At the first air, it somewhat troubled him.
(LEPIDUS
  Observe you?
ARRUNTIUS   Nothing. Riddles. Till I see
  Sejanus struck, no sound thereof strikes me.)   505
POMPONIUS
  I like it not. I muse he'd not attempt
  Somewhat against him in the Consulship,
  Seeing the people 'gin to favour him.
TERENTIUS
  He doth repent it, now; but he's employed
  Pagonianus after him: and he holds   510
  That correspondence, there, with all that are
  Near about Cæsar, as no thought can pass
  Without his knowledge, thence, in act to front him.
POMPONIUS
  I gratulate the news.
LACO   But, how comes Macro
  So in trust, and favour, with Caligula?   515
POMPONIUS
  O sir, he has a wife; and the young Prince
  An appetite: he can look up, and spy

495 *off* edd. (Q, F of)   498 MINUTIUS edd. (Q, F MAR.)
503 *air* news   506 *muse* imagine
514 *gratulate* welcome   LACO edd. (Q, F MAC.)

517f. *look up . . . his sleeps.* He can turn a blind eye to things near him, and
    has trained his senses to ignore what is going on.

Flies in the roof, when there are fleas in bed;
And hath a learnèd nose to assure his sleeps.
Who, to be favoured of the rising sun,   520
Would not lend little of his waning moon?
'Tis the safe'st ambition. Noble Terentius.

TERENTIUS
The night grows fast upon us. At your service.   [*Exeunt*]

CHORUS—OF MUSICIANS

[Act V, Scene i]

[Sejanus' house. Enter] SEJANUS

SEJANUS
Swell, swell, my joys: and faint not to declare
Yourselves, as ample, as your causes are.
I did not live, till now; this my first hour:
Wherein I see my thoughts reached by my power.
But this, and grip my wishes. Great, and high,   5
The world knows only two, that's Rome, and I.
My roof receives me not; 'tis air I tread:
And, at each step, I feel my advancèd head
Knock out a star in heav'n! Reared to this height,
All my desires seem modest, poor and slight,   10
That did before sound impudent: 'tis place,
Not blood, discerns the noble, and the base.
Is there not something more, than to be Cæsar?
Must we rest there? It irks, t'have come so far,
To be so near a stay. Caligula,   15
Would thou stood'st stiff, and many, in our way.
Winds lose their strength, when they do empty fly,
Unmet of woods or buildings; great fires die,
That want their matter to withstand them: so,
It is our grief, and will be our loss, to know   20

---

15 *stay* enforced stop

---

5 *grip my wishes.* Only let my power reach my thoughts, and I shall obtain
  my desires.
7 *My roof receives me not.* Sejanus thinks of himself as risen above his
  'house'; the image continues and completes a sequence which began at
  I, 225 ('One, and his house, receives') and continued in Macro's speech,
  III, 748–749 ('It is no uncouth thing/To see fresh buildings from old
  ruins spring') and Agrippina's (IV, 35), who sees the relation of this
  image to Sejanus' deed at Spelunca (IV, 55, 61). It is another example
  of interplay of language and action.

Our power shall want opposites; unless
The gods, by mixing in the cause, would bless
Our fortune with their conquest. That were worth
Sejanus' strife: durst fates but bring it forth.

[Enter] TERENTIUS, [SERVUS]

TERENTIUS
  Safety, to great Sejanus.
SEJANUS   Now, Terentius?   25
TERENTIUS
  Hears not my lord the wonder?
SEJANUS   Speak it, no.
TERENTIUS
  I meet it violent in the people's mouths,
  Who run, in routs, to Pompey's theatre,
  To view your statue: which, they say, sends forth
  A smoke, as from a furnace, black, and dreadful.   30
SEJANUS
  Some traitor hath put fire in: (you, go see.)
  And let the head be taken off, to look
  What 'tis—[*Exit* SERVUS] some slave hath practised an
                        imposture,
  To stir the people. How now? why return you?

[Enter] SATRIUS, NATTA, [SERVUS]
To them

SATRIUS
  The head, my lord, already is ta'en off,   35
  I saw it: and, at opening, there leapt out
  A great, and monstrous serpent!
SEJANUS   Monstrous! why?
  Had it a beard? and horns? no heart? a tongue
  Forked as flattery? looked it of the hue,
  To such as live in great men's bosoms? was   40
  The spirit of it Macro's?
NATTA   May it please
  The most divine Sejanus, in my days,
  (And by his sacred fortune, I affirm it)
  I have not seen a more extended, grown
  Foul, spotted, venomous, ugly —

33 *imposture* deception

---

34 Such a quick return of the servant is unreasonable, but Satrius' knowledge of Sejanus' order is equally so. The present arrangement assumes
  that Satrius and Natta have met the servant as he left Sejanus' house,
  and told him what they have already learned.

SEJANUS   O, the fates!   45
  What a wild muster's here of attributes,
  T'express a worm, a snake?
TERENTIUS   But how that should
  Come there, my lord!
SEJANUS   What! and you too, Terentius?
  I think you mean to make't a prodigy
  In your reporting?
TERENTIUS   Can the wise Sejanus   50
  Think heav'n hath meant it less?
SEJANUS   O, superstition!
  Why, then the falling of our bed, that broke
  This morning, burdened with the populous weight
  Of our expecting clients, to salute us;
  Or running of the cat, betwixt our legs,   55
  As we set forth unto the Capitol,
  Were prodigies.
TERENTIUS   I think them ominous!
  And, would they had not happened. As, today,
  The fate of some your servants! who, declining
  Their way, not able, for the throng, to follow,   60
  Slipped down the Gemonies, and broke their necks!
  Besides, in taking your last augury,
  No prosperous bird appeared, but croaking ravens
  Flagged up and down: and from the sacrifice
  Flew to the prison, where they sat, all night,   65
  Beating the air with their obstreperous beaks!
  I dare not counsel, but I could entreat
  That great Sejanus would attempt the gods,
  Once more, with sacrifice.
SEJANUS   What excellent fools
  Religion makes of men? Believes Terentius   70
  (If these were dangers, as I shame to think them)
  The gods could change the certain course of fate?
  Of, if they could, they would (now, in a moment)
  For a beef's fat, or less, be bribed t'invert
  Those long decrees? Then think the gods, like flies,   75
  Are to be taken with the steam of flesh,
  Or blood, diffused about their altars: think
  Their power as cheap, as I esteem it small.
  Of all the throng, that fill th'Olympian hall,
  And (without pity) lade poor Atlas' back,   80

52 *bed* couch or sofa   54 *expecting* awaiting (Latin *expecto*)
59 *declining* departing from   64 *Flagged* flew unsteadily
75 *long* old

I know not that one deity, but Fortune;
To whom, I would throw up, in begging smoke,
One grain of incense: or whose ear I'd buy
With thus much oil. Her, I, indeed, adore;
And keep her grateful image in my house,   85
Sometimes belonging to a Roman king,
But, now called mine, as by the better style:
To her, I care not, if (for satisfying
Your scrupulous fant'sies) I go offer. Bid
Our priest prepare us honey, milk, and poppy,   90
His masculine odours, and night vestments: say,
Our rites are instant, which performed, you'll see
How vain, and worthy laughter, your fears be.   [*Exeunt*]

                    [*Enter*] COTTA, POMPONIUS

COTTA
    Pomponius! whither in such speed?
POMPONIUS   I go
    To give my lord Sejanus notice—
COTTA   What?   95
POMPONIUS
    Of Macro.
COTTA   Is he come?
POMPONIUS   Entered but now
    The house of Regulus.
COTTA   The opposite Consul?
POMPONIUS
    Some half hour since.
COTTA   And, by night too! stay, sir;
    I'll bear you company.
POMPONIUS   Along, then—   [*Exeunt*]

                    [**Act V, Scene ii**]

            [*Regulus' house. Enter*] MACRO, REGULUS, [SERVUS]

MACRO
    'Tis Cæsar's will, to have a frequent Senate.   100
    And therefore must your edit lay deep mulct

85 *grateful* beneficent   86 *Sometimes* previously
100 *frequent* fully attended, frequented   101 *mulct* fine

---

91 *masculine odours*. 'A somewhat strange epithet in our tongue, but
    proper to the thing: for they were only masculine odours, which were
    offered to the altars' (Jonson, note to *Part of King James' Entertainment
    in Passing to his Coronation*; he goes on to cite classical authorities).

On such, as shall be absent.
REGULUS   So it doth.
   Bear it my fellow Consul to adscribe.
MACRO
   And tell him it must early be proclaimed;
   The place, Apollo's temple.   [*Exit* SERVUS]
REGULUS   That's remembered.   105
MACRO
   And at what hour?
REGULUS   Yes.
MACRO   You do forget
   To send one for the Provost of the watch?
REGULUS
   I have not: here he comes.

[*Enter* LACO]

MACRO   Gracinus Laco,
   You are a friend most welcome: by, and by,
   I'll speak with you. (You must procure this list   110
   Of the Prætorian cohorts, with the names
   Of the Centurions, and their Tribunes.
REGULUS   Ay.)
MACRO
   I bring you letters, and a health from Cæsar—
LACO
   Sir, both come well.
MACRO   (And hear you, with your note,
   Which are the eminent men, and most of action.   115
REGULUS
   That shall be done you too.)
MACRO   Most worthy Laco,
                    The Consul goes out
   Cæsar salutes you. (Consul! death, and furies!
   Gone now?) the argument will please you, sir.
   (Hough! Regulus? The anger of the gods
   Follow his diligent legs, and overtake 'em,   120
                        Returns
   In likeness of the gout.) O, good my lord,
   We lacked you present; I would pray you send
   Another to Fulcinius Trio, straight,
   To tell him, you will come, and speak with him:
   (The matter we'll devise) to stay him, there,   125
   While I, with Laco, do survey the watch.

103 *adscribe* subscribe
116 s.d. *The Consul* Regulus

What are your strengths, Gracinus?
LACO   Seven cohorts.
                        Goes out again
MACRO
  You see, what Cæsar writes: and (— gone again?
  He's sure a vein of Mercury in his feet)
  Knew you, what store of the Prætorian soldiers   130
  Sejanus holds, about him, for his guard?
LACO
  I cannot the just number: but, I think,
  Three centuries.
MACRO   Three? good.
LACO   At most, not four.
MACRO
  And who be those Centurions?
LACO   That the Consul
  Can best deliver you.
MACRO   (When he's away: 135
  Spite, on his nimble industry.) Gracinus,
  You find what place you hold, there, in the trust
  Of royal Cæsar?
LACO   Ay, and I am—
MACRO   Sir,
  The honours, there proposed, are but beginnings
  Of his great favours.
LACO   They are more—
MACRO   I heard him   140
  When he did study, what to add—
LACO   My life,
  And all I hold—
MACRO   You were his own first choice;
  Which doth confirm as much, as you can speak:
  And will (if we succeed) make more—Your guards
  Are seven cohorts, you say?
LACO   Yes.
MACRO   Those we must   145
  Hold still in readiness, and undischarged.
LACO
  I understand so much. But how it can—
MACRO
  Be done without suspicion, you'll object?
                        Returns
REGULUS
  What's that?

132 *just* exact

LACO   The keeping of the watch in arms,
  When morning comes.
MACRO   The Senate shall be met, and set   150
  So early, in the temple, as all mark
  Of that will be avoided.
REGULUS   If we need,
  We have commission, to possess the palace;
  Enlarge Prince Drusus, and make him our chief.
MACRO
  (That secret would have burnt his reverend mouth,   155
  Had he not spit it out, now:) by the gods,
  You carry things too—let me borrow a man,
  Or two, to bear these—that of freeing Drusus,
  Cæsar projected as the last, and utmost;
  Not else to be remembered.

                    [*Enter* SERVI]

REGULUS   Here are servants.   160
MACRO
  These to Arruntius, these to Lepidus,
  This bear to Cotta, this to Latiaris.
  If they demand you of me: say, I have ta'en
  Fresh horse, and am departed. You (my lord)
  To your colleague, and be you sure, to hold him   165
  With long narration, of the new fresh favours,
  Meant to Sejanus, his great patron; I,
  With trusted Laco, here, are for the guards:
  Then, to divide. For, night hath many eyes,
  Whereof, though most do sleep, yet some are spies. [*Exeunt*] 170

[Act V, Scene iii]

[*Sejanus' house. Enter*] PRÆCONES, FLAMEN, MINISTRI,
[TUBICINES, TIBICINES,] SEJANUS, TERENTIUS, SATRIUS,
            [NATTA,] *etc.*

PRÆCO
  Be all profane far hence; fly, fly far off:
  Be absent far. Far hence be all profane.

  Tubicines, Tibicines sound, while the Flamen washeth

FLAMEN
  We have been faulty, but repent us now,
  And bring pure hands, pure vestments, and pure minds.

154 *Enlarge* set free

1 MINISTER
   Pure vessels.
2 MINISTER   And pure offerings.
3 MINISTER   Garlands pure.   175
FLAMEN
   Bestow your garlands: and (with reverence) place
   The vervin on the altar.
PRÆCO   Favour your tongues.
While they sound again, the Flamen takes of the honey,
with his finger, and tastes, then ministers to all the rest: so
of the milk, in an earthen vessel, he deals about; which done,
he sprinkleth, upon the altar, milk; then imposeth the honey,
and kindleth his gums, and after censing about the altar
placeth his censer thereon, into which they put several
branches of poppy, and the music ceasing, proceed
FLAMEN
   Great mother Fortune, queen of human state,
   Rectress of action, arbitress of fate,
   To whom all sway, all power, all empire bows,   180
   Be present, and propitious to our vows.
PRÆCO
   Favour it with your tongues.
1 MINISTER
   Be present, and propitious to our vows.
   Accept our offering, and be pleased, great goddess.
TERENTIUS
   See, see, the image stirs!
SATRIUS   And turns away!   185
NATTA
   Fortune averts her face!
FLAMEN   Avert, you gods,
   The prodigy. Still! still! Some pious rite
   We have neglected. Yet! heav'n, be appeased.
   And be all tokens false, or void, that speak
   Thy present wrath.
SEJANUS   Be thou dumb, scrupulous priest: 190
   And gather up thyself, with these thy wares,

177 *vervin* verbena, boughs used in sacrifices
190 *scrupulous* meticulous

---

177 *Favour your tongues.* Cf. V, 182, *Favour it with your tongues.* Jonson's
   note to Q explains the meaning of the phrase ('be silent') and the
   alternative translations of *favete linguis*, the first regarding the noun as
   dative, the second (correctly) as ablative. The note gives examples from
   Virgil and Ovid, and cites sixteenth-century scholarly authority.
   s.d. *gums.* Aromatics used in the censer.

Which I, in spite of thy blind mistress, or
Thy juggling mystery, religion, throw
Thus, scornèd on the earth. Nay, hold thy look
Averted, till I woo thee, turn again;   195
And thou shalt stand, to all posterity,
Th'eternal game, and laughter, with thy neck
Writhed to thy tail, like a ridiculous cat.
Avoid these fumes, these superstitious lights,
And all these cosening ceremonies: you,   200
Your pure, and spicèd conscience. [*Exeunt* FLAMEN,
                          ATTENDANTS] I, the slave,
And mock of fools, (scorn on my worthy head)
That have been titled, and adored a god,
Yea, sacrificed unto, myself, in Rome,
No less than Jove: and I be brought, to do   205
A peevish giglot rites? Perhaps, the thought,
And shame of that made Fortune turn her face,
Knowing herself the lesser deity,
And but my servant. Bashful queen, if so,
Sejanus thanks thy modesty. Who's that?   210

               [*Enter*] POMPONIUS, MINUTIUS

POMPONIUS
   His fortune suffers, till he hears my news:
   I have waited here too long. Macro, my lord—
SEJANUS
   Speak lower, and withdraw.
TERENTIUS   Are these things true?
MINUTIUS
   'Thousands are gazing at it, in the streets.
SEJANUS
   What's that?
TERENTIUS   Minutius tells us here, my lord,   215
   That, a new head being set upon your statue,
   A rope is since found wreathed about it! and,
   But now, a fiery meteor, in the form
   Of a great ball, was seen to roll along
   The troubled air, where yet it hangs, unperfect, 220
   The amazing wonder of the multitude!

197 *game* object of scorn
198 *Writhed to thy tail* turned backwards
200 *cosening* duping
201 *spicèd* overdelicate
206 *giglot* a wanton woman (read 'to do rites unto a peevish giglot')
220 *unperfect* without having completed its flight

SEJANUS

　No more. That Macro's come, is more than all!

TERENTIUS

　Is Macro come?

POMPONIUS　　　　I saw him.

TERENTIUS　　　　　　　Where? with whom?

POMPONIUS

　With Regulus.

SEJANUS　　　　Terentius—

TERENTIUS　　　　　　My lord?

SEJANUS

　Send for the Tribunes, we will straight have up　　　225
　More of the soldiers, for our guard. [*Exit* TERENTIUS]
　　　　　　　　　　　　　　　　　　　　Minutius,
　We pray you, go for Cotta, Latiaris,
　Trio the Consul, or what Senators
　You know are sure, and ours. [*Exit* MINUTIUS] You, my
　　　　　　　　　　　　　　　　　　good Natta,
　For Laco, Provost of the watch. [*Exit* NATTA] Now,
　　　　　　　　　　　　　　　　　　Satrius,　　230
　The time of proof comes on. Arm all our servants,
　And without tumult. [*Exit* SATRIUS] You, Pomponius,
　Hold some good correspondence, with the Consul,
　Attempt him, noble friend. [*Exit* POMPONIUS] These
　　　　　　　　　　　　　　　　　　things begin
　To look like dangers, now, worthy my fates.　　　235
　Fortune, I see thy worst: let doubtful states,
　And things uncertain hang upon thy will:
　Me surest death shall render certain still.
　Yet, why is, now, my thought turned toward death,
　Whom fates have let go on, so far, in breath,　　　240
　Unchecked, or unreproved? I, that did help
　To fell the lofty cedar of the world,
　Germanicus; that, at one stroke, cut down
　Drusus, that upright elm; withered his vine;
　Laid Silius, and Sabinus, two strong oaks,　　　245
　Flat on the earth; besides, those other shrubs,
　Cordus, and Sosia, Claudia Pulchra,
　Furnius, and Gallus, which I have grubbed up;
　And since, have set my axe so strong, and deep
　Into the root of spreading Agrippine;　　　250
　Lopped off, and scattered her proud branches, Nero,

233 *correspondence* conversation
244 *vine* his wife Livia; the elm and vine was a marriage image

Drusus, and Caius too, although replanted;
If you will, destinies, that, after all,
I faint, now, ere I touch my period;
You are but cruel: and I already have done   265
Things great enough. All Rome hath been my slave;
The Senate sat an idle looker on,
And witness of my power; when I have blushed,
More, to command, than it to suffer; all
The Fathers have sat ready, and prepared,   260
To give me empire, temples, or their throats,
When I would ask 'em; and (what crowns the top)
Rome, Senate, people, all the world have seen
Jove, but my equal: Cæsar, but my second.
'Tis then your malice, fates, who (but your own)   265
Envy, and fear, t'have any power long known.   [*Exit*]

[Enter] TERENTIUS, TRIBUNES

TERENTIUS
Stay here: I'll give his lordship, you are come.

[Enter] MINUTIUS, COTTA, LATIARIS
They confer their letters

MINUTIUS
Marcus Terentius, pray you tell my lord,
Here's Cotta, and Latiaris.
TERENTIUS   Sir, I shall.
COTTA
My letter is the very same with yours;   270
Only requires me to be present there,
And give my voice, to strengthen his design.
LATIARIS
Names he not what it is?
COTTA   No, nor to you.
LATIARIS
'Tis strange, and singular doubtful!
COTTA   So it is?
It may be all is left to lord Sejanus.   275

[Enter] NATTA, LACO
To them

NATTA
Gentlemen, where's my lord?
TRIBUNE   We wait him here.

252 *Caius* Caligula
267 *give* tell

COTTA
  The Provost Laco? what's the news?
LATIARIS   My lord—

[Enter] SEJANUS
To them

SEJANUS
  Now, my right dear, noble, and trusted friends;
  How much I am a captive to your kindness!
  Most worthy Cotta, Latiaris; Laco,   280
  Your valiant hand; and gentlemen, your loves.
  I wish I could divide myself unto you;
  Or that it lay, within our narrow powers,
  To satisfy for so enlargèd bounty.
  Gracinus, we must pray you, hold your guards   285
  Unquit, when morning comes. Saw you the Consul?
MINUTIUS
  Trio will presently be here, my lord.
COTTA
  They are but giving order for the edict,
  To warn the Senate.
SEJANUS   How! the Senate?
LATIARIS   Yes.
  This morning, in Apollo's temple.
COTTA   We   290
  Are charged, by letter, to be there, my lord.
SEJANUS
  By letter? Pray you let's see!
LATIARIS   Knows not his lordship!
COTTA
  It seems so!
SEJANUS   A Senate warned? without my knowledge?
  And on this sudden? Senators by letters
  Required to be there! who brought these?
COTTA   Macro.   295
SEJANUS
  Mine enemy! And when?
COTTA   This midnight.
SEJANUS   Time,
  With every other circumstance, doth give
  It hath some strain of engine in't! *[Enter]* SATRIUS
                                        How now?
SATRIUS
  My lord, Sertorius Macro is without,

286 *Unquit* undischarged

    Alone, and prays t'have private conference   300
    In business, of high nature, with your lordship,
    (He says to me) and which regards you much.
SEJANUS
    Let him come here.
SATRIUS   Better, my lord, withdraw,
    You will betray what store, and strength of friends
    Are now about you; which he comes to spy.   305
SEJANUS
    Is he not armed?
SATRIUS   We'll search him.
SEJANUS   No, but take,
    And lead him to some room, where you, concealed,
    May keep a guard upon us. [*Exit* SATRIUS] Noble Laco,
    You are our trust: and, till our own cohorts
    Can be brought up, your strengths must be our guard. 310
    Now, good Minutius, honoured Latiaris,
             He salutes them humbly
    Most worthy, and my most unwearied friends:
    I return instantly.   [*Exit* SEJANUS]
LACO   Most worthy lord!
COTTA
    His lordship is turned instant kind, me thinks,
    I have not observed it in him, heretofore.   315
1 TRIBUNE
    'Tis true, and it becomes him nobly.
MINUTIUS   I
    Am rapt withal.
2 TRIBUNE
            By Mars, he has my lives,
    (Were they a million) for this only grace.
LACO
    Ay, and to name a man!
LATIARIS   As he did me!
MINUTIUS
    And me!
LATIARIS   Who would not spend his life and fortunes,   320
    To purchase but the look of such a lord?
LACO
    He, that would nor be lord's fool, nor the world's.

318 *only* single

[Act V, Scene iv]

[*Another room in Sejanus' house. Enter*] SEJANUS, MACRO,
[SATRIUS]

SEJANUS
  Macro! most welcome, as most coveted friend!
  Let me enjoy my longings. When arrived you?
MACRO
  About the noon of night.
SEJANUS   Satrius, give leave.   [*Exit* SATRIUS]   325
MACRO
  I have been, since I came, with both the Consuls,
  On a particular design from Cæsar.
SEJANUS
  How fares it with our great, and royal master?
MACRO
  Right plentifully well; as, with a prince,
  That still holds out the great proportion   330
  Of his large favours, where his judgement hath
  Made once divine election: like the god,
  That wants not, nor is wearied to bestow
  Where merit meets his bounty, as it doth
  In you, already the most happy, and ere   335
  The sun shall climb the south, most high Sejanus.
  Let not my lord be amused. For, to this end
  Was I by Cæsar sent for, to the isle,
  With special caution to conceal my journey;
  And, thence, had my dispatch as privately   340
  Again to Rome; charged to come here by night;
  And, only to the Consuls, make narration
  Of his great purpose: that the benefit
  Might come more full, and striking, by how much
  It was less looked for, or aspired by you,   345
  Or least informèd to the common thought.

327 *particular design* private mission
337 *amused* amazed

---

325 *About the noon of night.* Herford and Simpson list contemporary
    imitators of this phrase, but Jonson was not the source, only an inter-
    mediary quoting Nonius' citation of Varro's *noctis circiter meridiem* (*De
    comp. doct.* 451, 9).
330f. *That still . . . his bounty.* That still extends the great quantity of his
    generous favours, to whom he formerly chose; like the god who lacks
    not bounty, and does not tire of giving it to the man who deserves it.

SEJANUS
   What may this be? part of my self, dear Macro!
   If good, speak out: and share with your Sejanus.
MACRO
   If bad, I should forever loathe myself,
   To be the messenger to so good a lord.   350
   I do exceed m'instructions, to acquaint
   Your lordship with thus much; but 'tis my venture
   On your retentive wisdom: and, because
   I would no jealous scruple should molest
   Or rack your peace of thought. For, I assure   355
   My noble lord, no Senator yet knows
   The business meant: though all, by several letters,
   Are warnèd to be there, and give their voices,
   Only to add unto the state, and grace
   Of what is purposed.
SEJANUS   You take pleasure, Macro,   360
   Like a coy wench, in torturing your lover.
   What can be worth this suffering?
MACRO   That which follows,
   The tribunicial dignity, and power:
   Both which Sejanus is to have this day
   Conferred upon him, and by public Senate.   365
SEJANUS
   Fortune, be mine again; thou hast satisfied
   For thy suspected loyalty.
MACRO   My lord,
   I have no longer time, the day approacheth,
   And I must back to Cæsar.
SEJANUS   Where's Caligula?
MACRO
   That I forgot to tell your lordship. Why,   370
   He lingers yonder, about Capreæ,
   Disgraced; Tiberius hath not seen him yet:
   He needs would thrust himself to go with me,
   Against my wish, or will, but I have quitted
   His forward trouble, with as tardy note   375
   As my neglect, or silence could afford him.
   Your lordship cannot now command me ought,
   Because, I take no knowledge that I saw you,
   But I shall boast to live to serve your lordship:
   And so take leave.
SEJANUS   Honest, and worthy Macro,   380

353 *retentive wisdom* wise secrecy
357 *several* separate

Your love, and friendship. Who's there? Satrius,
                                        [*Exit* MACRO]
Attend my honourable friend forth. O!
How vain, and vile a passion is this fear?
What base, uncomely things it makes men do?
Suspect their noblest friends, (as I did this)   385
Flatter poor enemies, entreat their servants,
Stoop, court, and catch at the benevolence
Of creatures, unto whom (within this hour)
I would not have vouchsafed a quarter-look,
Or piece of face? By you, that fools call gods,   390
Hang all the sky with your prodigious signs,
Fill earth with monsters, drop the scorpion down,
Out of the zodiac, or the fiercer lion,
Shake off the loosened globe from her long hinge,
Roll all the world in darkness, and let loose   395
Th'engagèd winds to turn up groves and towns;
When I do fear again, let me be struck
With forkèd fire, and unpitied die:
Who fears, is worthy of calamity.   [*Exit*]

[Act V, Scene v]

[*Same as scene iii. Enter*] POMPONIUS, REGULUS, TRIO
                    To the rest
POMPONIUS
   Is not my lord here?
TERENTIUS   Sir, he will be straight.   400
COTTA
   What news, Fulcinius Trio?
TRIO   Good, good tidings.
   (But, keep it to yourself) my lord Sejanus
   Is to receive this day, in open Senate,
   The tribunicial dignity.
COTTA   Is't true?
TRIO
   No words; not to your thought: but, sir, believe it.   405
LATIARIS
   What says the Consul?
COTTA   (Speak it not again,)
   He tells me, that today my lord Sejanus—
(TRIO
   I must entreat you Cotta, on your honour
   Not to reveal it.

389 *quarter-look* face almost averted   394 *hinge* axis of the earth

R—E

COTTA　　　　　　　On my life, sir.)
LATIARIS　　　　　　　　　Say.
COTTA
　Is to receive the tribunicial power.　　　　　　　　410
　But, as you are an honourable man,
　Let me conjure you, not to utter it:
　For it is trusted to me, with that bond.
LATIARIS
　I am Harpocrates.
TERENTIUS　　　Can you assure it?
POMPONIUS
　The Consul told it me, but keep it close.　　　　　415
MINUTIUS
　Lord Latiaris, what's the news?
LATIARIS　　　　　　　　I'll tell you,
　But you must swear to keep it secret

　　　　　　[*Enter*] SEJANUS
　　　　　　　To them

SEJANUS
　I knew the fates had on their distaff left
　More of our thread, than so.
REGULUS　　　　　　Hail, great Sejanus.
TRIO
　Hail, the most honoured.
COTTA　　　　　　　Happy.
LATIARIS　　　　　　　　High Sejanus.　　　420
SEJANUS
　Do you bring prodigies too?
TRIO　　　　　　　May all presage
　Turn to those fair effects, whereof we bring
　Your lordship news.
REGULUS　　　　　May't please my lord withdraw.
　　　　　　To some that stand by
SEJANUS
　Yes (I will speak with you, anon.)
TERENTIUS　　　　　　My lord,
　What is your pleasure for the Tribunes?
SEJANUS　　　　　　　Why,　　　425
　Let 'em be thanked, and sent away.
MINUTIUS　　　　　　My lord —
LACO
　Will't please your lordship to command me —
SEJANUS　　　　　　　No.

418f. A reference to the goddesses that wind the thread of men's lives.

You are troublesome.
MINUTIUS　　　　　　　　The mood is changed.
1 TRIBUNE　　　　　　　　　　　　　　　Not speak?
2 TRIBUNE
　Nor look?
LACO　　　　Ay. He is wise, will make him friends
　Of such, who never love, but for their ends.　　　[*Exeunt*]　430

[Act V, Scene vi]

[*The temple of Apollo. Enter*] ARRUNTIUS, LEPIDUS, *divers
　　　other* SENATORS *passing by them*

ARRUNTIUS
　Ay, go, make haste; take heed you be not last
　To tender your 'All hail', in the wide hall
　Of huge Sejanus: run, a Lictor's pace;
　Stay not to put your robes on; but, away,
　With the pale troubled ensigns of great friendship　　　435
　Stamped in your face! Now, Marcus Lepidus,
　You still believe your former augury?
　Sejanus must go downward? you perceive
　His wane approaching fast?
LEPIDUS　　　　　　　　Believe me, Lucius,
　I wonder at this rising!
ARRUNTIUS　　　　　　　　Ay, and that we　　　440
　Must give our suffrage to it? you will say,
　It is to make his fall more steep, and grievous?
　It may be so. But think it, they that can
　With idle wishes 'ssay to bring back time:
　In cases desperate, all hope is crime.　　　445
　See, see! what troops of his officious friends
　Flock to salute my lord! and start before
　My great, proud lord! to get a lordlike nod!
　Attend my lord, unto the Senate house!
　Bring back my lord! like servile ushers, make　　　450
　Way for my lord! proclaim his idol lordship,
　More than ten criers, or six noise of trumpets!
　Make legs, kiss hands, and take a scattered hair
　From my lord's eminent shoulder! See, Sanquinius!
　With his slow belly, and his dropsy! look,　　　455
　What toiling haste he makes! yet, here's another,

433 *Lictor's pace* rapidly
444 *'ssay* essay, attempt

Retarded with the gout, will be afore him!
Get thee Liburnian porters, thou gross fool,
To bear thy obsequious fatness, like thy peers.
They are met! The gout returns, and his great carriage.   460

LICTORS, CONSULS, SEJANUS, *etc., pass over the stage*

LICTOR
Give way, make place; room for the Consul.
SANQUINIUS   Hail,
Hail, great Sejanus.
HATERIUS   Hail, my honoured lord.
ARRUNTIUS
We shall be marked anon, for our not-hail.
LEPIDUS
That is already done.
ARRUNTIUS   It is a note
Of upstart greatness, to observe, and watch   465
For these poor trifles, which the noble mind
Neglects, and scorns.
LEPIDUS   Ay, and they think themselves
Deeply dishonoured, where they are omitted,
As if they were necessities, that helped
To the perfection of their dignities: 470
And hate the men, that but refrain 'em.
ARRUNTIUS   O!
There is a farther cause of hate. Their breasts
Are guilty, that we know their obscure springs,
And base beginnings: thence the anger grows. On. Follow.
                                        [*Exeunt*]

[*Enter*] MACRO, LACO

MACRO
When all are entered, shut the temple doors;   475
And bring your guards up to the gate.
LACO   I will.
MACRO
If you shall hear commotion in the Senate,
Present yourself: and charge on any man
Shall offer to come forth.
LACO   I am instructed.   [*Exeunt*]

[*Enter*] THE SENATE. HATERIUS, TRIO, SANQUINIUS, COTTA,
REGULUS, SEJANUS, POMPONIUS, LATIARIS, LEPIDUS,
ARRUNTIUS, PRÆCONES, LICTORES, [PRÆTORS, SENATORS]

463 *marked* noticed (cf. V, 501)

HATERIUS
　How well his lordship looks today!
TRIO　　　　　　　　　　　　As if　　　　　　480
　He had been born, or made for this hour's state.
COTTA
　Your fellow Consul's come about, me thinks?
TRIO
　Ay, he is wise.
SANQUINIUS　　　　Sejanus trusts him well.
TRIO
　Sejanus is a noble, bounteous lord.
HATERIUS
　He is so, and most valiant.
LATIARIS　　　　　　　And most wise.　　　　485
1 SENATOR
　He's everything.
LATIARIS　　　　Worthy of all, and more
　Than bounty can bestow.
TRIO　　　　　　　　This dignity
　Will make him worthy.
POMPONIUS　　　　　Above Cæsar.
SANQUINIUS　　　　　　　　　Tut,
　Cæsar is but the rector of an isle,
　He of the Empire.
TRIO　　　　　　　Now he will have power　　　490
　More to reward, than ever.
COTTA　　　　　　　　Let us look
　We be not slack in giving him our voices.
LATIARIS
　Not I.
SANQUINIUS Nor I.
COTTA　　　　　The readier we seem
　To propagate his honours, will more bind
　His thought, to ours.
HATERIUS　　　　　I think right, with your lordship.　　495
　It is the way to have us hold our places.
SANQUINIUS
　Ay, and get more.
LATIARIS　　　　　More office, and more titles.
POMPONIUS
　I will not lose the part, I hope to share
　In these his fortunes, for my patrimony.

487f. *dignity . . . worthy* with a quibble on Latin *dignus*, 'worthy'
499 *patrimony* inheritance

LATIARIS
  See, how Arruntius sits, and Lepidus.   500
TRIO
  Let 'em alone, they will be marked anon.
1 SENATOR
  I'll do with others.
2 SENATOR   So will I.
3 SENATOR   And I.
  Men grow not in the State, but as they are planted
  Warm in his favours.
COTTA   Noble Sejanus!
HATERIUS
  Honoured Sejanus!
LATIARIS   Worthy, and great Sejanus!   505
ARRUNTIUS
  Gods! how the sponges open, and take in!
  And shut again! look, look! is not he blest
  That gets a seat in eye-reach of him? more,
  That comes in ear, or tongue-reach? O, but most,
  Can claw his subtle elbow, or with a buzz   510
  Fly-blow his ears.
PRÆTOR   Proclaim the Senate's peace;
  And give last summons by the edict.
PRÆCO   Silence:
  In name of Cæsar, and the Senate. Silence.
  'Memmius Regulus, and Fulcinius Trio, Consuls, these
  present kalends of June, with the first light, shall hold a   515
  Senate, in the temple of Apollo Palatine, all that are Fathers,
  and are registered Fathers, that have right of entering the
  Senate, we warn, or command, you be frequently
  present, take knowledge the business is the Common-
  wealth's, whosoever is absent, his fine, or mulct, will be   520
  taken, his excuse will not be taken.'
TRIO
  Note, who are absent, and record their names.
REGULUS
  Fathers Conscript. May, what I am to utter,
  Turn good, and happy, for the Commonwealth.
  And thou Apollo, in whose holy house   525
  We here are met, inspire us all, with truth,
  And liberty of censure, to our thought.
  The majesty of great Tiberius Cæsar
  Propounds to this grave Senate, the bestowing

527 *censure* judgment

Upon the man he loves, honoured Sejanus,   530
The tribunicial dignity, and power;
Here are his letters, signed with his signet:
What pleaseth now the Fathers to be done?
SENATORS
Read, read 'em, open, publicly, read 'em.
COTTA
Cæsar hath honoured his own greatness much,   535
In thinking of this act.
TRIO   It was a thought
Happy, and worthy Cæsar.
LATIARIS   And the lord,
As worthy it, on whom it is directed!
HATERIUS
Most worthy!
SANQUINIUS   Rome did never boast the virtue
That could give envy bounds, but his: Sejanus—   540
1 SENATOR
Honoured, and noble!
2 SENATOR   Good, and great Sejanus!
ARRUNTIUS
O, most tame slavery, and fierce flattery!
PRÆCO   Silence.

The Epistle is read

'Tiberius Cæsar to the Senate, greeting.
If you, Conscript Fathers, with your children, be in health,
it is abundantly well: we with our friends here, are so.   545
The care of the Commonwealth, howsoever we are removed
in person, cannot be absent to our thought; although, often-
times, even to princes most present, the truth of their own
affairs is hid: than which, nothing falls out more miserable
to a state, or makes the art of governing more difficult. But 550
since it hath been our easeful happiness to enjoy both the
aids, and industry of so vigilant a Senate, we profess to have
been the more indulgent to our pleasures, not as being careless of our office, but rather secure of the necessity. Neither
do these common rumours of many, and infamous libels,   555
published against our retirement, at all afflict us; being born
more out of men's ignorance, than their malice: and will,
neglected, find their own grave quickly; whereas too sensibly
acknowledged, it would make their obloquy ours. Nor do
we desire their authors (though found) be censured, since   560

554 *necessity* the Senate's aid and industry

in a free state (as ours) all men ought to enjoy both their
minds, and tongues free.'
(ARRUNTIUS
  The lapwing, the lapwing.)
'Yet, in things, which shall worthily, and more near concern
the majesty of a prince, we shall fear to be so unnaturally   565
cruel to our own fame, as to neglect them. True it is,
Conscript Fathers, that we have raised Sejanus, from
obscure, and almost unknown gentry,'
(SENATORS
  How! how!)
'to the highest, and most conspicuous point of greatness,   570
and (we hope) deservingly; yet, not without danger: it
being a most bold hazard in that sovereign, who, by his
particular love to one, dares adventure the hatred of all his
other subjects.'
(ARRUNTIUS
  This touches, the blood turns.)   575
'But we affy in your loves, and understandings, and do no
way suspect the merit of our Sejanus to make our favours
offensive to any.'
(SENATORS
  O! good, good.)
'Though we could have wished his zeal had run a calmer course   580
against Agrippina, and our nephews, howsoever the open-
ness of their actions, declared them delinquents; and, that he
would have remembered, no innocence is so safe, but it
rejoiceth to stand in the sight of mercy: the use of which in
us, he hath so quite taken away, toward them, by his loyal   585
fury, as now our clemency would be thought but wearied
cruelty, if we should offer to exercise it.'
(ARRUNTIUS
  I thank him, there I looked for't. A good fox!)
'Some there be, that would interpret this his public severity
to be particular ambition; and that, under a pretext of   590
service to us, he doth but remove his own lets: alleging the
strengths he hath made to himself, by the Prætorian soldiers,
by his faction in Court, and Senate, by the offices he holds
himself, and confers on others, his popularity, and depen-
dants, his urging (and almost driving) us to this our   595
unwilling retirement, and lastly his aspiring to be our son-
in-law.'

563 *lapwing* said to divert predators from its nest by calling afar
576 *affy in* have trust in (cf. affidavit)

(SENATORS
   This's strange!
ARRUNTIUS
   I shall anon believe your vultures, Marcus.)
   'Your wisdoms, Conscript Fathers, are able to examine, and   600
   censure these suggestions. But, were they left to our ab-
   solving voice, we durst pronounce them, as we think them,
   most malicious.'
(SENATORS
   O, he has restored all, list.)
   'Yet, are they offered to be averred, and on the lives of the   605
   informers. What we should say, or rather what we should
   not say, lords of the Senate, if this be true, our gods, and
   goddesses confound us if we know! Only, we must think, we
   have placed our benefits ill: and conclude, that, in our
   choice, either we were wanting to the gods, or the gods to us.'   610
              The Senators shift their places.
(ARRUNTIUS
   The place grows hot, they shift.)
   'We have not been covetous, honourable Fathers, to change;
   neither is it now, any new lust that alters our affection, or
   old loathing: but those needful jealousies of state, that warn
   wiser princes, hourly, to provide their safety; and do teach   615
   them how learned a thing it is to beware of the humblest
   enemy; much more of those great ones, whom their own
   employed favours have made fit for their fears.'
(1 SENATOR
   Away.
2 SENATOR Sit farther.
COTTA   Let's remove—
ARRUNTIUS
   Gods! how the leaves drop off, this little wind!)   620
   'We therefore desire, that the offices he holds, be first seized
   by the Senate; and himself suspended from all exercise of
   place, or power —'
(SENATORS
   How!
SANQUINIUS By your leave.
ARRUNTIUS   Come, porpoise, (where's Haterius?
   His gout keeps him most miserably constant.)   625
   Your dancing shows a tempest.)
SEJANUS   Read no more.
REGULUS
   Lords of the Senate, hold your seats: read on.

624 *porpoise* its activity was said to warn of storm

SEJANUS
   These letters, they are forged.
REGULUS   **A guard, sit still.**
        Laco enters with the guards
ARRUNTIUS
   There's change.
REGULUS   Bid silence, and read forward.
PRÆCO   Silence —
   'and himself suspended from all exercise of place, or power,   630
   but till due and mature trial be made of his innocency,
   which yet we can faintly apprehend the necessity, to doubt.
   If, Conscript Fathers, to your more searching wisdoms,
   there shall appear farther cause (or of farther proceeding,
   either to seizure of lands, goods, or more —) it is not our   635
   power that shall limit your authority, or our favour, that
   must corrupt your justice: either were dishonourable in
   you, and both uncharitable to ourself. We would willingly
   be present with your counsels in this business, but the
   danger of so potent a faction (if it should prove so) forbids   640
   our attempting it: except one of the Consuls would be
   entreated for our safety, to undertake the guard of us home,
   then we should most readily adventure. In the meantime,
   it shall not be fit for us to importune so judicious a Senate,
   who know how much they hurt the innocent, that spare the   645
   guilty: and how grateful a sacrifice, to the gods, is the life
   of an ingrateful person. We reflect not, in this, on Sejanus
   (notwithstanding, if you keep an eye upon him — and there
   is Latiaris a Senator, and Pinnarius Natta, two of his most
   trusted ministers, and so professed, whom we desire not   650
   to have apprehended) but as the necessity of the cause
   exacts it.'
REGULUS
   A guard on Latiaris.
ARRUNTIUS   O, the spy!
   The reverend spy is caught, who pities him?
   Reward, sir, for your service: now, you've done   655
   Your property, you see what use is made?
   Hang up the instrument.
SEJANUS   Give leave.
LACO   Stand, stand,
   He comes upon his death, that doth advance
   And inch toward my point.

651 *apprehended* edd. (Q, F apprênded, after Latin *apprêndo*)
656 *property* function

SEJANUS   Have we no friends here?
ARRUNTIUS
  Hushed. Where now are all the hails, and acclamations?   660

[Enter] MACRO

MACRO
  Hail, to the Consuls, and this noble Senate.
SEJANUS
  Is Macro here? O, thou art lost, Sejanus.
MACRO
  Sit still, and unaffrighted, reverend Fathers.
  Macro, by Cæsar's grace, the new-made Provost,
  And now possessed of the Prætorian bands,   665
  An honour late belonged to that proud man,
  Bids you, be safe: and to your constant doom
  Of his deservings, offers you the surety
  Of all the soldiers, Tribunes, and Centurions,
  Received in our command.
REGULUS   Sejanus, Sejanus,   670
  Stand forth, Sejanus.
SEJANUS   Am I called?
MACRO   Ay, thou,
  Thou insolent monster, art bid stand.
SEJANUS   Why, Macro,
  It hath been otherwise, between you, and I?
  This court that knows us both, hath seen a difference,
  And can (if it be pleased to speak) confirm,   675
  Whose insolence is most.
MACRO   Come down Typhœus,
  If mine be most, lo, thus I make it more;
  Kick up thy heels in air, tear off thy robe,
  Play with thy beard, and nostrils. Thus 'tis fit,
  (And no man take compassion of thy state)   680
  To use th'ingrateful viper, tread his brains
  Into the earth.
REGULUS   Forbear.
MACRO   If I could lose
  All my humanity now, 'twere well to torture
  So meriting a traitor. Wherefore, Fathers,
  Sit you amazed, and silent? and not censure   685
  This wretch, who in the hour he first rebelled
  'Gainst Cæsar's bounty, did condemn himself?

---

667 *constant doom* loyal judgment

Phlegra, the field, where all the sons of earth
Mustered against the gods, did ne'er acknowledge
So proud, and huge a monster.

REGULUS   Take him hence.   690
And all the gods guard Cæsar.

TRIO   Take him hence.

HATERIUS
Hence.

COTTA
To the dungeon with him.

SANQUINIUS   He deserves it.

1 SENATOR
Crown all our doors with bays.

SANQUINIUS   And let an ox
With gilded horns, and garlands, straight be led
Unto the Capitol.

HATERIUS   And sacrificed   695
To Jove, for Cæsar's safety.

TRIO   All our gods
Be present still to Cæsar.

COTTA   Phœbus.

SANQUINIUS   Mars.

HATERIUS
Diana.

SANQUINIUS Pallas.

2 SENATOR   Juno, Mercury,
All guard him.

MACRO   Forth, thou prodigy of men. [*Exit* SEJANUS *guarded*]

COTTA
Let all the traitor's titles be defaced.   700

TRIO
His images, and statues be pulled down.

HATERIUS
His chariot wheels be broken.

ARRUNTIUS   And the legs

---

688 *Phlegra.* The form *P'hlegra* appears in both states of Q and of F. It may
    nevertheless be an error, perhaps caused by the movement of the in-
    verted comma from before aphetic '*Gainst* in the previous line, which
    lacks the mark in Q. More probably it is a hypercorrect spelling inven-
    ted by Jonson to show that the Greeks pronounced *ph* as an aspirated *p*
    (as in 'ha*ph*azard'), even though Macro, as a Roman, would have pro-
    nounced it *f*.

693, 698 In one or both of these lines the temptation to read *Senator* for
    Sanquinius (i.e., SEN. for F SAN.) is strong.

Of the poor horses, that deservèd naught,
Let them be broken too.
LEPIDUS   O, violent change,
And whirl of men's affections!
ARRUNTIUS   Like, as both   705
Their bulks and souls were bound on Fortune's wheel,
And must act only with her motion!
                [*Exeunt, leaving*] LEPIDUS, ARRUNTIUS
LEPIDUS
Who would depend upon the popular air,
Or voice of men, that have today beheld
(That which if all the gods had foredeclared,   710
Would not have been believed) Sejanus' fall?
He, that this morn rose proudly, as the sun?
And, breaking through a mist of clients' breath,
Came on as gazed at, and admired, as he
When superstitious Moors salute his light!   715
That had our servile nobles waiting him
As common grooms; and hanging on his look,
No less than human life on destiny!
That had men's knees as frequent, as the gods;
And sacrifices, more, than Rome had altars: 720
And this man fall! fall? Ay, without a look,
That durst appear his friend; or lend so much
Of vain relief, to his changed state, as pity!
ARRUNTIUS
They, that before like gnats played in his beams,
And thronged to circumscribe him, now not seen!   725
Nor deign to hold a common seat with him!
Others, that waited him unto the Senate,
Now, inhumanly ravish him to prison!
Whom (but this morn) they followed as their lord,
Guard through the streets, bound like a fugitive!   730
Instead of wreaths, give fetters; strokes, for stoops:
Blind shame, for honours; and black taunts, for titles!
Who would trust slippery chance?
LEPIDUS   They, that would make
Themselves her spoil: and foolishly forget,
When she doth flatter, that she comes to prey.   735
Fortune, thou hadst no deity, if men
Had wisdom: we have placed thee so high,
By fond belief in thy felicity.
                Shout within

715 *Moors.* The reference is to Roman belief that Libyans worshipped the
    sun.

SENATORS
The gods guard Cæsar. All the gods guard Cæsar.

[Enter] MACRO, REGULUS, SENATORS

MACRO
Now great Sejanus, you that awed the State,   740
And sought to bring the nobles to your whip,
That would be Cæsar's tutor, and dispose
Of dignities, and offices! that had
The public head still bare to your designs,
And made the general voice to echo yours!   745
That looked for salutations, twelve score off,
And would have pyramids, yea, temples reared
To your huge greatness! now, you lie as flat,
As was your pride advanced.
REGULUS   Thanks, to the gods.
SENATORS
And praise to Macro, that hath savèd Rome.   750
Liberty, liberty, liberty. Lead on,
And praise to Macro, that hath savèd Rome.
                    [Exeunt leaving] ARRUNTIUS, LEPIDUS
ARRUNTIUS
I prophesy, out of this Senate's flattery,
That this new fellow, Macro, will become
A greater prodigy in Rome, than he   755
That now is fall'n.

                    [Enter] TERENTIUS

TERENTIUS   O you, whose minds are good,
And have not forced all mankind, from your breasts;
That yet have so much stock of virtue left,
To pity guilty states, when they are wretched:
Lend your soft ears to hear, and eyes to weep   760
Deeds done by men, beyond the acts of furies.
The eager multitude, (who never yet
Knew why to love, or hate, but only pleased
T'express their rage of power) no sooner heard
The murmur of Sejanus in decline,   765
But with that speed, and heat of appetite,
With which they greedily devour the way

757 *mankind* humanity   760 *soft* sympathetic

---

746 *twelve score off.* Two hundred forty yards, a common length for a shot
     in archery. Macro's taste for archery imagery (cf. III, 720f.) is an
     example of Jonson's 'poetic', as distinguished from 'dramatic' or
     'psychological', characterization.

To some great sports, or a new theatre,
They filled the Capitol, and Pompey's cirque;
Where, like so many mastiffs, biting stones,   770
As if his statues now were sensive grown
Of their wild fury, first, they tear them down:
Then fastening ropes, drag them along the streets,
Crying in scorn, 'this, this was that rich head
Was crowned with garlands, and with odours, this   775
That was in Rome so reverencèd! Now
The furnace, and the bellows shall to work
The great Sejanus crack, and piece, by piece,
Drop in the founder's pit!'
LEPIDUS   O, popular rage!
TERENTIUS
The whilst, the Senate, at the temple of Concord,   780
Make haste to meet again, and thronging cry,
'Let us condemn him, tread him down in water,
While he doth lie upon the bank; away:'
Where some, more tardy, cry unto their bearers,
'He will be censured ere we come, run knaves;'   785
And use that furious diligence, for fear
Their bondmen should inform against their slackness,
And bring their quaking flesh unto the hook:
The rout, they follow with confusèd voice,
Crying, they are glad, say they could ne'er abide him;   790
Enquire, what man he was? what kind of face?
What beard he had? what nose? what lips? protest,
They ever did presage he'd come to this:
They never thought him wise, nor valiant: ask
After his garments, when he dies? what death?   795
And not a beast of all the herd demands,
What was his crime? or, who were his accusers?
Under what proof, or testimony, he fell?
'There came' (says one) 'a huge, long, worded letter
From Capreæ against him.' 'Did there so?'   800
O, they are satisfied, no more.
LEPIDUS   Alas!
They follow fortune, and hate men condemned,
Guilty, or not.

769 *cirque* theatre
771 *sensive* capable of feeling sensation

___

779 *founder's pit.* Where broken pieces of metal were melted down to be re-
    cast; Sejanus' statue, which figured early in the play, embodies in the
    action the philosophical theme of mutability. (For the source, see
    Appendix A.)

ARRUNTIUS   But, had Sejanus thrived
  In his design, and prosperously oppressed
  The old Tiberius, then, in that same minute   805
  These very rascals, that now rage like furies,
  Would have proclaimed Sejanus Emperor.
LEPIDUS
  But what hath followed?
TERENTIUS   Sentence, by the Senate;
  To lose his head: which was no sooner off,
  But that, and th'unfortunate trunk were seized   810
  By the rude multitude; who not content
  With what the forward justice of the State,
  Officiously had done, with violent rage
  Have rent it limb, from limb. A thousand heads,
  A thousand hands, ten thousand tongues, and voices,   815
  Employed at once in several acts of malice!
  Old men not staid with age, virgins with shame,
  Late wives with loss of husbands, mothers of children,
  Losing all grief in joy of his sad fall,
  Run quite transported with their cruelty!   820
  These mounting at his head, these at his face,
  These digging out his eyes, those with his brain,
  Sprinkling themselves, their houses, and their friends;
  Others are met, have ravished thence an arm,
  And deal small pieces of the flesh for favours;   825
  These with a thigh; this hath cut off his hands;
  And this his feet; these fingers, and these toes;
  That hath his liver; he his heart: there wants
  Nothing but room for wrath, and the place for hatred!
  What cannot oft be done, is now o'erdone.   830
  The whole, and all of what was great Sejanus,
  And next to Cæsar did possess the world,
  Now torn, and scattered, as he needs no grave,
  Each little dust covers a little part:

---

812 *forward* eager

---

821 *mounting.* Herford and Simpson believe this line corrupt and this word
'impossible'; Whalley quoted a suggested emendation to 'minting', i.e.,
'aiming', little improvement though it seems to make. The passage
follows fairly closely Claudius' description of the dismemberment of
another tyrant, Rufinus (who perished more than three centuries after
Sejanus; Jonson's employment of *In Rufinum* illustrates again his
artistic synchronization of history), but the Latin throws no light on
these words. Perhaps the line is to be understood 'some jumping at his
newly-removed head as it was hurled above the throng, some others
particularly at his face'.

So lies he nowhere, and yet often buried!   835

[*Enter*] NUNTIUS

ARRUNTIUS
More of Sejanus?
NUNTIUS   Yes.
LEPIDUS   What can be added?
We know him dead.
NUNTIUS   Then, there begin your pity.
There is enough behind, to melt ev'n Rome,
And Cæsar into tears: (since never slave
Could yet so highly offend, but tyranny,   840
In torturing him, would make him worth lamenting.)
A son, and daughter, to the dead Sejanus,
(Of whom there is not now so much remaining
As would give fastening to the hangman's hook)
Have they drawn forth for farther sacrifice;   845
Whose tenderness of knowledge, unripe years,
And childish silly innocence was such,
As scarce would lend them feeling of their danger:
The girl so simple, as she often asked,
Where they would lead her? for what cause they dragged
                                                        her? 850
Cried, she would do no more. That she could take
Warning with beating. And because our laws
Admit no virgin immature to die,
The wittily, and strangely cruel Macro,
Delivered her to be deflowered, and spoiled,   855
By the rude lust of the licentious hangman,
Then, to be strangled with her harmless brother.
LEPIDUS
O, act, most worthy hell, and lasting night,
To hide it from the world!
NUNTIUS   Their bodies thrown
Into the Gemonies, (I know not how,   860
Or by what accident returned) the mother,
Th'expulsèd Apicata, finds them there;
Whom when she saw lie spread on the degrees,
After a world of fury in herself,
Tearing her hair, defacing of her face,   865
Beating her breasts, and womb, kneeling amazed,
Crying to heaven, then to them; at last,
Her drownèd voice got up above her woes:

854 *wittily* cleverly
862 *expulsèd* exiled
863 *degrees* steps

And with such black, and bitter execrations,
(As might affright the gods, and force the sun   870
Run backward to the east, nay, make the old
Deformèd chaos rise again, t'o'erwhelm
Them, us, and all the world) she fills the air;
Upbraids the heavens with their partial dooms,
Defies their tyrannous powers, and demands,   875
What she, and those poor innocents have transgressed,
That they must suffer such a share in vengeance,
Whilst Livia, Lygdus, and Eudemus live,
Who, (as she says, and firmly vows, to prove it
To Cæsar, and the Senate) poisoned Drusus?   880

LEPIDUS
Confederates with her husband?

NUNTIUS   Ay.

LEPIDUS   Strange act!

ARRUNTIUS
And strangely opened: what says now my monster,
The multitude? they reel now? do they not?

NUNTIUS
Their gall is gone, and now they 'gin to weep
The mischief they have done.

ARRUNTIUS   I thank 'em, rogues!   885

NUNTIUS
Part are so stupid, or so flexible,
As they believe him innocent; all grieve:
And some, whose hands yet reek with his warm blood,
And grip the part which they did tear of him,
Wish him collected, and created new.   890

LEPIDUS
How Fortune plies her sports, when she begins
To practise 'em! pursues, continues, adds!
Confounds, with varying her impassioned moods!

ARRUNTIUS
Dost thou hope Fortune to redeem thy crimes?
To make amends, for thy ill placèd favours,   895
With these strange punishments? Forbear, you things,
That stand upon the pinnacles of state,
To boast your slippery height; when you do fall,
You pash yourselves in pieces, ne'er to rise:
And he that lends you pity, is not wise.   900

874 *partial dooms* unjust judgements
899 *pash* smash

TERENTIUS

   Let this example move th'insolent man,
Not to grow proud, and careless of the gods:
It is an odious wisdom, to blaspheme,
Much more to slighten, or deny their powers.
For, whom the morning saw so great, and high,   905
Thus low, and little, 'fore the even doth lie.   [*Exeunt*]

THE END

Appendix A

JUVENAL'S TENTH SATIRE

Jonson's many near and remote sources for *Sejanus* are listed and, in many cases, reprinted in the editions of W. D. Briggs, and Herford and Simpson. It would be pointless to reproduce them all here, but to afford some illustration of the kind of use he made of them, the relevant lines from Juvenal's tenth *Satire*, with references to the play, are given below in literal prose translation.

Jonson's method in assimilating Juvenal's poem, to which he turned for the end of Sejanus' life where Tacitus' *Annals* had an awkward gap, is very far from mere translation, *verbatim* and *seriatim*. Instead he breaks the material up so that it forms part of speeches by Sabinus, Arruntius, the Senators, Lepidus, and Terentius, drawing it into the dialogue of his dramatic poem. In Juvenal, the historical narrative is only one of several chosen to illustrate the moral of the last two lines; in Jonson the moral is the same, but the narrative is expanded from other sources to fill the entire poem.

(*Satire* X, 56–77)	(*Sejanus*)
Some men excessive power, a thing of great envy, hurls down; the long page, embellished with their honours, overwhelms them. Down come their statues,	V. 701 f.
following the rope, the smashing axe breaks the wheels of their chariots and the legs of their innocent horses; now the flames hiss, now	V. 776 f.
by the bellows and the forge the head adored by the populace is burnt and mighty Sejanus crackles, and from the face once second in	I. 217
the whole world, they make jugs, basins, frying	V. 779
pans and pots. Put laurel over your door, lead	V. 693 f.
a bull covered with chalk to the Capitol. Sejanus is dragged by the hook, a spectacle, everyone rejoices: 'What lips he had, what	V. 792 f.
a face!' 'Never, believe me, did I like the man.' 'But under what accusation did he fall? Who was the accuser? By what evidence, by what witness was he condemned?' 'Nothing of that kind; a long and wordy letter came from Capreæ.' 'Good enough, I ask no more.' And what does the mob of Remus say? They follow Fortune as always	V. 801 f.

and hate the condemned. The same crowd, if
Fortune had favoured her man, if a secret blow
had felled the Emperor, in the same hour would
have called Sejanus their Augustus.
(85–88)

'Let us run with haste and, as he lies on the   V. 781 f.
bank, let us trample Cæsar's enemy.' 'But let
the servants see, that none of them may bear
witness against his master, and drag him
trembling into court.'
(92–94)

'[If you were Sejanus, you would want] to be
thought the tutor of a prince, sitting on a   IV. 403
narrow ledge in Capreæ with his crowd of   IV. 380
Chaldees.'
(103–107)

Therefore you agree that Sejanus did not know   V. 896 f.
what things to seek; for he who sought too many
honours and had too much wealth, was building
the many stories of a high tower, whence the
fall would be greater, and horrible the crash   V. 442
of utter ruin.
(365–366)

You would have no deity, Fortune, if we had   V. 736 f.
but wisdom; it is we, we who make you a goddess
and put you in heaven.

Appendix B

GLOSSARY OF CLASSICAL NAMES

Names marked thus* are the subject of a separate entry.

Ædiles Administrative officials below Prætors*.

Æmilian Of the family of Manius Æmilius Lepidus*, who restored the 'Basilica Pauli', built by his grandfather.

Æsculapius God of healing.

Afer, Cnæus Domitius Orator who, in history, won the favour of Tiberius* by prosecuting Claudia Pulchra*.

Afranius, Lucius Consul* and legate under Pompey*, with whose party he was condemned for treachery.

Agrippina, Vipsania ('major') Widow of Germanicus*, granddaughter of Augustus*; starved to death in Pandataria* A.D. 33.

Alcides Hercules*.

Alexander 'The Great' of Macedon, adventurer and conqueror, died aged thirty-three, probably of fever.

Antium Modern Anzio, south of Rome; in classical times a fashionable resort known for its temples.

Antonius, Marcus Marc Anthony, soldier and follower of Julius Cæsar*. His letters are quoted by Suetonius.

Apicata Wife of Sejanus* whom he sent away during his intrigue with Livia*. After his death, Apicata revealed what she knew of the murder of Drusus senior*.

Apicius, Marcus Gavius Wealthy gourmet under Augustus* and Tiberius*.

Apollo God, especially of music, archery, prophecy, and medicine; his temple on the Palatine hill was erected by Augustus*.

Arruntius, Lucius Highly respected Senator*, committed suicide in A.D. 37 when accused by Macro*.

Atlas Mythological Titan, tricked into holding the world on his back.

Augusta, Livia Widow of Augustus* and mother of Tiberius*.

Augustus Cæsar, Caius Octavius Stepfather and adopted father of Tiberius*; Augusta* was his second wife. He died at Nola* and was declared a god of the State.

Bibaculus, Marcus Furius Author of a poem on Julius Cæsar's* wars in Gallia* which like his *Epigrams* has not survived.

Brutus, Marcus Junius Follower of Pompey*, pardoned by Julius Cæsar*, whom he conspired against with Cassius* and slew. He committed suicide after the battle of Philippi*. Nothing is known of his 'pleadings'.

Cæsar See under Augustus; Caius; Caligula; Julius; Tiberius.

Caius Cæsar Grandson of Augustus*, first husband of Livia*.

Caligula, Caius Cæsar Youngest son of Germanicus*, joined Tiberius* on Capreæ* (historically, after Sejanus'* death); next in succession to the throne after Drusus senior* and his own brothers, he may have brought about the death of Tiberius* with the aid of Macro*. He died violently in A.D. 41.

Campania The region of middle Italy containing Capua*, Nola*, Naples and the island of Capreæ*.

Capitol One of the hills of Rome, the site of many temples.

Capreæ Modern Capri, an island near Naples whence Tiberius* retired and Caligula* fled.

Capua City in Campania* linked with Rome by the Via Appia, modern Santa Maria di Capua Vetere (not modern Capua).

Cassius Longinus, Caius Follower of Pompey* pardoned after the Civil War by Julius Cæsar*, whom he later conspired against with Brutus* and slew. He committed suicide at the battle of Philippi*.

Castor (i) A famous gladiator. (ii) Mythological son of Jupiter* and twin brother of Pollux*.

Cato Uticensis, Marcus Porcius Statesman who opposed Julius Cæsar* and followed Pompey* into exile, where he committed suicide.

Catullus Roman poet; his abuse of Julius Cæsar is in *Poems* 11, 29, 54, 57, 93.

Centurion Commander of a century*.

Century Division of troops made up of one hundred men.

Chaldees Astrologers; the science of predicting a person's destiny by the position of the stars at his birth was cultivated in Chaldea.

Cicero, Marcus Tullius Roman statesman who wrote, amongst many others, a work in favour of Cato*, answered by Julius Cæsar's* *Anticato*; both are lost.

Cithera An error, followed by Jonson, for Cythnos (modern Kythnos) in the Cyclades islands off Greece, near Gyaros (the 'other isle') where Silanus* was first exiled.

Claudia Pulchra Cousin (not niece) of Agrippina*, prosecuted by Afer* for adultery with Furnius* and for plotting to poison Tiberius*.

Cohort Division of troops containing six centuries*.

Colossus Vast statue of a man straddling the entrance to the harbour of Rhodes*.

Concord Goddess, personification of civil harmony.

Consul Supreme magistrate in Rome, of whom two were appointed by the Emperor to hold office for several months.

Cordus, Aulus Cremutius Historian; committed suicide in A.D. 25. His books were burnt, but some fragments were saved by his daughter.

Cotta, Maximus Messalinus Marcus Aurelius Senator* and Consul*, enemy of Lepidus*, later disgraced for remarks about Caligula*.

Cupid Mythological son of Venus*, he shot his victims with arrows which caused them to fall in love.

Diana Goddess, huntress.

Dictator Civil and military leader with authority not subject to veto or appeal.

Drusus (junior), Julius Cæsar Second son of Germanicus*, starved to death in the palace two years after Sejanus'* execution.

Drusus Cæsar (senior) Son of Tiberius* by his first wife, second husband of his own first cousin, Tiberius' niece Livia*.

Eudemus Physician, accomplice of Sejanus* and Livia* in the murder of Drusus senior*. He was accused by Apicata*, tortured and executed.

Fathers Conscript Really 'Fathers and Conscripts', Senators* of the usual sort and others 'enrolled' to make up the number to 600 after the exile of the Tarquin party.

Flamen Priest.

Fortune Goddess of chance in late Rome; her iconography for Jonson's age is discussed in the Introduction and in Shakespeare's *Henry V*, III.vi.

Fundane Relating to the area about modern Fondi, half way between Rome and Naples.

Furies Spirits of vengeance for wrong.

Furnius Put to death for adultery with Claudia Pulchra*.

Gallia The Roman province Gaul, about the same area as modern France.

Gallus, Caius Asinius Married the divorced first wife of Tiberius*, who sentenced him and starved him to death.

Gauls Natives of Gallia*.

Gemonies 'The Gemonian steps . . . on which bodies were thrown to dishonour them, sometimes dragged by the hangman's hook' (Jonson's note to IV, 309).

Germanicus, Julius Cæsar Nephew of Tiberius*, who later adopted him; husband of Agrippina*. He may have died of poison.

Germany The Roman province of Germania, roughly equivalent to modern Germany and south central Europe.

Gracinus See Laco.

Harpocrates God of silence and secrecy.

Haterius, Quintus Senator* and orator, the object of Tiberius'* remark (also applied by Jonson to Shakespeare) 'Haterius needs a brake'.

Hecatomb Sacrifice of a hundred oxen.

Hell and Elysium Places of abode in the after-life: Hell an underworld not necessarily painful, Elysium the Isles of the Blessed.

Hercules Hero, sometimes worshipped as a god, noted for his great strength and ability to avert evil.

Horace (Quintus Horatius Flaccus) Roman poet, author of, amongst other things, *Satires* and a discussion of *The Art of Poetry*, including drama; for a time a follower of Brutus*.

Jove Jupiter, the supreme deity.

Julius See Cæsar; Posthumus.

Julius Cæsar, Caius Became Consul* in league with Pompey* and established the army with which he warred in Gallia*, returning across the Rubicon and driving Pompey into exile. The Pompeians conducted a peripheral war with him, but he was the subject of extraordinary honours in Rome. He was murdered in a conspiracy led by Brutus* and Cassius*.

Juno Wife of Jove* and supreme goddess.

Jupiter Jove*.

Kalends First day of the month.

Laco, Græcinus ('Gracinus') Provost* of the night-watch at the crisis of Sejanus'* career.

Latiaris, Latinius (Lucanius) Friend, not — historically — a relative, of Sabinus*, whom he betrayed; denounced in Tiberius'* letter to the Senate*.

Lepidus, Manius Æmilius ('Marcus') A responsible elder statesman. (Jonson's error about his prænomen follows Lipsius.)

Liburnians Central European slaves who acted as court messengers.
Lictores Attendants on Roman magistrates who carried the fasces.
Linceus Argonaut, known for the power of his sight.
Livia (*Livilla*) Niece of Tiberius*, daughter of Nero Drusus, sister of Germanicus*, married first to Caius Cæsar*, grandson of Augustus*, and second to Drusus senior*. In history she died before Sejanus*.
Lucius See Arruntius.
Lygdus Handsome young eunuch, cupbearer to Drusus senior*; as such he would taste his master's wine to guard against poison.

Macedon See Alexander.
Macro, Nævius Sertorius Tiberius'* agent in the overthrow of Sejanus*, whom he followed as Provost* of the Prætorian* guard; died under persecution of Caligula*, whom he helped to the throne.
Marcus See Lepidus.
Mars God of war.
Mercury Messenger of the gods, noted for swiftness.
Messalla Corvinus Next in command to Brutus* and Cassius* at Philippi*; wrote a history of the civil war.
Ministri (singular *Minister*) Attendants.
Minutius Thermus Minor associate of Sejanus*, after whose death he was condemned.

Natta, Pinnarius Client of Sejanus* who accused Cordus*.
Nero, Julius Cæsar Eldest son of Germanicus*, next in succession to the throne after Drusus senior*; exiled to Pontia* and starved to death there. (Not to be confused with C. Julius Cæsar* or with Nero the arsonist.)
Nola Town in Campania* near Naples, still known by this name.
Nuntius Messenger.

Œdipus Greek who solved the riddle of the Sphinx*.
Olympia Mountain dwelling-place of the gods.
Opsius, Marcus Conspirator with Latiaris* and Rufus* in the betrayal of Sabinus*.

Pagonianus (*Paconianus*), *Sextius* Helper of Sejanus* in the plot against Caligula*; later strangled in prison.
Pallas Athene Goddess of wisdom, often shown armed.
Pandataria See Pontia.

Parthian Citizen of central Asia minor.

Pergamum Modern Bergama, Turkey.

Philippi Scene in northern Greece of the battle in which Antonius* defeated Brutus* and Cassius*.

Phlegra Pallene, in Macedonia, where the struggle between the giants, including Typhœus*, and the gods took place (cf. IV, 270, note).

Phœbus Personification of the sun. (See also Apollo.)

Plancina Wife of Piso, with him suspected of a hand in the death of Germanicus*.

Pollio, Asinius Poet, historian and statesman, of whose writing fragments only remain.

Pollux Twin brother of Castor*. The pair functioned as protective deities.

Pompey, Cnæus General, first associate and later opponent of Julius Cæsar*, by whom he was defeated at Pharsalus.

Pomponius Minor confederate of Sejanus*.

Pontia Modern Ponza, like Pandataria an island near Naples employed as a place of confinement.

Posthumus, Julius Lover of Augusta's* friend Mutilia Prisca*, through whom Sejanus* influenced Tiberius*.

Præcones (singular *Præco*) Heralds.

Prætor State official below Consuls* and above Ædiles*, twelve in number at this time.

Prætorian The imperial bodyguard, the garrison for Rome.

Prisca, Mutilia Mistress of Julius Posthumus* and intimate friend of Augusta*.

Provost Commander of the Prætorian* guard.

Regulus, Livineus Friend of Agrippina* mentioned II, 220; not the same as the next entry.

Regulus, Publius Memmius Consul* in the year of Sejanus'* death.

Rhadamanth Mythological judge of the dead.

Rhodes Island of Tiberius'* exile during Augustus'* reign; the Colossus* stood at the harbour entrance.

Rufus, Petilius Betrayer, with Opsius* and Latiaris*, of Sabinus*.

Sabinus, Titius Friend of Germanicus*, betrayed by Latiaris* and executed for treason.

Sacrovir Leader of a rebellion in Gallia* in A.D. 21.

Sanquinius Senator*, later accuser of Arruntius*.

Satrius Secundus Client of Sejanus* who accused Cordus*, but he may have been amongst those who divulged Sejanus' conspiracy.

Scipio, Metellus Father-in-law of Pompey*.

Sejanus, Lucius Ælius Son of Sejus Strabo*, became with his father commander of the Prætorian* guard and subsequently an influence on Tiberius*. He lost control of the guard when Tiberius became suspicious, and was condemned in A.D. 31.

Senate, Senators Chief council of state with a membership of 600, largely hereditary, partly by election and imperial nomination.

Servus (plural *Servi*) Servant, attendant.

Sestertia (singular *Sestertium*) A thousand *sestertii*. A Roman private soldier earned just under a *sestertium* a year, minus his keep.

Sicambrians (*Sugambrians*) A tribe in Germany*.

Silanus, Caius Exiled in A.D. 22 for plundering Asia.

Silius, Caius Served under Germanicus*, defeated Sacrovir*, killed himself (but not in the Senate*) when accused of treason and extortion.

Sinon Greek who duped the Trojans into accepting the wooden horse.

Sosia Galla Wife of Caius Silius* and friend of Agrippina*.

Spain Roman province of Hispania, roughly the Iberian peninsula.

Spelunca Modern Sperlonga, between Rome and Naples.

Sphinx Monster which kept Thebes under its power until Œdipus* solved its riddle.

Strabo, Sejus Lucius A knight from Vulsinii*, Provost* of the Prætorian* guard and father of Sejanus*.

Terentius, Marcus Friend of Sejanus*, but later acquitted of guilt. The last lines of the play are his.

Tiber The principal river of Rome.

Tiberius Cæsar Stepson and adopted son of Augustus*, father of Drusus senior*, uncle of Germanicus*. At the time of the play in his sixties.

Tibicines Flautists.

Titus Livius The Roman historian Livy; wrote under Augustus*.

Tribune One of the six commanding officers of a Roman legion; also, a civilian official with wide powers, including veto.

Trio, Lucius Fulcinius Conspirator with Sejanus*, whom he aided as Consul*; the association forced him to commit suicide in A.D. 35.

Tubicines Trumpeters.

Typhœus One of the giants who sought to overthrow Zeus (cf. IV, 270, note) and failed.

Urgulania Friend of Augusta.*

Varro, Lucius Visellius Consul* suborned by Sejanus* in the prosecution of Silius*.

Venus Goddess of love; wife of Vulcan*, mother of Cupid*, mistress of Mars*.

Vertumnus God of the changing year.

Vulcan Armourer of the gods. He trapped his wife Venus* with her lover Mars* in a net of wires.

Vulsinii Modern Bolsena, between Rome and Florence. Birthplace of Sejanus*, it paid particular honour to Nortia, the Etruscan equivalent of Fortune*.

Printed in Great Britain by Cox & Wyman Limited
London · Reading · Fakenham